THE UNBROKEN LINE

D1594695

THE
UNBROKEN
LINE

THE UNTOLD STORY OF GRIDIRON GREATS AND THEIR STRUGGLE TO SAVE PROFESSIONAL FOOTBALL

BILLY JOE DUPREE & SPENCER KOPF

iUniverse, Inc.
New York   Bloomington

Contributors

Noel Brown
Tony Davis
Fred Dean
Joe DeLamielleure
Anthony Dickerson
John Hogan
Barry Horn
Jerri Mote
Scott Murray
Robert Newhouse
and
Norm Wells

Copyright © 2010 by Billy Joe DuPree and Spencer Kopf
All rights reserved. No part of this book may be used or reproduced by any means,
graphic, electronic, or mechanical, including photocopying, recording, taping or by
any information storage retrieval system without the written permission of the publisher
except in the case of brief quotations embodied in critical articles and reviews.

Because of the dynamic nature of the Internet, any Web addresses or links contained in this
book may have changed since publication and may no longer be valid. The views expressed
in this work are solely those of the author and do not necessarily reflect the views of the
publisher, and the publisher hereby disclaims any responsibility for them.

ISBN: 978-1-4401-9160-2 (dj)
ISBN: 978-1-4401-9159-6 (sc)
ISBN: 978-1-4401-9158-9 (e-book)

Printed in the United States of America

iUniverse rev. date: 4/09/2010

iUniverse books may be ordered through booksellers or by contacting:
iUniverse
1663 Liberty Drive
Bloomington, IN 47403
www.iuniverse.com
1-800-Authors (1-800-288-4677)

To the memory of Lamar Hunt:
For his love of the game and the players who play it

Contents

Acknowledgments

Many retired NFL players who played in the Sixties, Seventies and Eighties influenced this book. Acknowledgment of those who have been neglected by the union, acknowledgement of their contribution and present status needs to be first and foremost. My wife and family, for their love and support. My High School Coach Darnell Cowan, Michigan State University Head Football Coach Duffy Daugherty, Dallas Cowboys Head Coach Tom Landry and Coach Gene Stallings, for their guidance. Former Judge Spencer Kopf, who had the courage at 32 to challenge the status quo of the NFL and the Players Union, for his assistance in writing this book. Coach Mike Ditka and Joe DeLamielleure. Both men have exposed the plight of retired NFL players. Robert Newhouse, for his courage during the strike of 1982.

Billy Joe DuPree

The players, for football. Billy Joe DuPree, for his vision, courage, determination and friendship. My son Jared, for his contributions during the long haul that was this book. Dave Smith, for his guidance and friendship during those tough days; he is the gold standard for journalism. Former Oklahoma City University Assistant Sports Information Director, Doug Todd, my old friend and confidant who is missed every day. Robert Newhouse, a true man of principles. Were it not for his courage to speak the truth under the most adverse circumstances, the outcome of the 1982 strike might have been diametrically different. Joe and Gerri DeLamielleure, for their encouragement and confidence in the project and their devotion to retired players. Tony Davis and John Hogan, for their immeasurable assistance and for their devotion to retired players of the NFLPA. Rich Hoshino, Noel Brown and Fred Dean, who know why. Scott Murray and Barry Horn, for their professional guidance and friendship. Norm Wells and Anthony Dickerson for their devotion and resolve for the project and for me. Doug Cosbie, Don Smerek, John Fitzgerald, Danny Spradlin, Steve Wilson, Larry Bethea, Emmitt Smith, Jay Saldi and Drew Pearson. Jerri Mote for her kindness to me and the players. To awesome Lisa Litchfield and my dear friend and confidant, Don Wilmarth. Larry "Double" Lange, for always being there even when I didn't know it. Coach A. E. "Abe" Lemons and Coach Paul Hansen, who both convinced me that it's not the size of the dog in the fight, it's the size of the fight in the dog. Edward "Ted" Wachendorfer, Jim Burnham, Hon. David Finn, Justice Robert M. Hill, Judge Harold Entz, James A. Rolfe, William T. Hill, Jr., Hon. Ron Chapman, and Hon. Richard Mays, for all their help, advice and friendship. Justin Ware, for his introduction. Kirkland Tibbels, for his expertise and guidance. Glenn Selig and Justin Herndon for their devotion to the project and their assistance. Jack Haaker, Lamar

Hunt, Richard Huebner, R.P. "Bob" Moore, Johnny Washington, my son Jordan and all my other Kappa Sigma brothers. AEKDB. George Kalinsky, for his guidance throughout my life, without which I would never have been able to face that task in 1982 or co-author this book today. Finally, my mother Shirley Kopf, for being my greatest fan in sports and in life.

Spencer W. Kopf

Preface

This story needed to be told, not only to set the record straight as to what really happened during those tenuous weeks in the fall of 1982, but to bring an end to the continuous misrepresentations of the people entrusted to protect the players that they were hired to serve.

When you tell a tale like this one, names are inevitably dropped and fantastic situations are inevitably portrayed; in the world of sports and sports representation, that's just the way it is. We hope the reader will enjoy this true adventure.... We are proud to have been a part of the struggle for the just treatment of athletes—proud to tell the world of sports what really happened.

Billy Joe DuPree and Spencer Kopf
January 2010

Foreword

Although most people know me as that strong-willed football player and as the head coach with those tough, emotionally charged mannerisms, many know that I am also an admirer of the underdog—the one who battles against a seemingly unbeatable foe. I was instilled with the belief that winners never quit and quitters never win—that, most importantly, "anybody can beat anybody on a given day."

When people think of historical turning points, they usually attribute these to the courage and personal fortitude of certain individuals who have either been thrust into the line of fire by circumstance or those who have decided to undertake an apparently insurmountable task with nothing but their principles and backbone to guide them. When the Bears won the Super Bowl, it was the result of tenacious teamwork and guts, and all we had to do was defeat another team. We certainly never would have won if we'd had to battle within our own team as well. What *The Unbroken Line* reveals is that players in 1982 had to battle the people who were supposed to be guiding them. This is the worst kind of foe.

This book gives a lucid, concise, and in-depth assessment of the inadequacies and inabilities of the professional football league union leadership back in the early eighties.

The timing of the release of this book, coupled with the eventual labor relations talks (or possible strike) with the NFL management council in the next two years, is compelling. It is even more compelling in the light of the $28 million verdict rendered by a California jury in 2009 against the National Football League Players Association (NFLPA) and Players, Inc., for breaching their trust to many of their members. In the face of that disgrace, this book enlightens the public and the active union members to the union leadership's blatant misconduct: these leaders have ignored the court and jury's finding by allowing those who breached their fiduciary duty to remain employed or in high positions of influence.

This is substantiated by the very fact that the new executive director of the NFLPA has chosen to continue business as usual since his election in May 2009 by retaining the same individuals the California court had discredited. The contents and information within *The Unbroken Line* establish for the reader the importance of bringing to the attention of the common man the unthinkable reality that even our sports heroes are vulnerable to those who are consciously indifferent to the American principles of fair play and job integrity. The reader will meet the people who sacrificed much and risked all for the well-being of their teammates and friends.

Billy Joe and Spencer bring to the forefront certain "freight train realities" that have been discovered over the years regarding the eyebrow-raising conduct and business dealings of the NFLPA union leadership in their capacity of running the NFLPA and the operation and direction of monies of the NFLPA marketing company known as Players, Inc. In this book, the events flow from one player's perspective to another's; it is a quiver full of many short stories with profound characters, each with strong beliefs and idiosyncrasies that captivate the imagination. You really feel like you're in the room with them as they reveal that behind those closed doors in November 1982, a maverick group of football players, led by Billy Joe DuPree (Pro Bowl, NFC All-Pro with the Dallas Cowboys) and Spencer Kopf (a former municipal judge, respected sports attorney, and analyst for the *Dallas Morning News*), enacted their version of the Statue of Liberty play—they fooled them all. This story may have been set in motion by the arrogant conduct of the participants of the labor talks and an irascible arbitrator, but it was finished by a perfect plan with a perfectly coached team of NFL football players led by a feisty sports-industry-savvy attorney. The story unfolds with the tension of a close football game inside two minutes in the fourth quarter, and ends with the true winners crossing the goal line in victory.

Through the actual disability benefits cases of former players, prominent attorney John Hogan wraps up this book by eloquently exposing the questionable procedures used by NFLPA leaders and League representatives serving on the Bert Bell/Pete Rozelle NFL Retirement Plan Board in determining a fair and just finding of facts. Some of these cases are so deplorable that one wonders how, in a society drenched with rules and regulations to protect the hurt and injured in our nation, wounded warriors of the gridiron could be so shabbily treated and forgotten.

Finally, this book exposes the need for the complete renovation of the football players' union—a complete overhaul: a new NFLPA constitution, unbiased union leadership that can have *no* economic interests permitted, industry standard salaries and performance bonuses only, the hiring of a third-party administrator to oversee economic decisions, and the establishment of disability panels with professional committee members sitting in judgment on matters where they have no personal ties to union membership or the team they work for. This book reinforces the need for such an overhaul. We must protect the game; we must protect the players who played, play, and will play it; we must protect the *entire* union membership.

This book establishes that the present union leadership is satisfied with taking little or no action concerning legitimate efforts in the future care or economic well-being of its retired brethren. The token gesture of the recent appointment of a retired player/member of the NFLPA to sit at the negotiating table in the upcoming labor talks with the owners is mere window dressing to placate former players.

Billy Joe and his fellow stouthearted men's careful description of the current message being delivered by the NFLPA Executive Director DeMaurice Smith tells us all that outside of the politically correct rhetoric, the intended movement to rectify the deplorable pension plan, and the other promised benefits to those retired players of yesteryear will remain mere rhetoric.

We have realized that our weakness is ourselves, the professional football players. The active player of today is the retired player of tomorrow. We are *all* teammates in the game and business of professional football. We can control at least a semblance of our destiny as it pertains to the protection of ourselves and our fellow players, present and past. This book is a call to action telling us that and more. It is a panoramic view of the wrong that has been done and continues to be done to those who have done everything but wrong.

The message of *The Unbroken Line* is well taken. It should be a model reading regarding the formation and importance of lifelong relationships based on principle, created from a unified goal that has continued these many years based on the love, devotion, and everlasting friendship shared by that cadre of players. They saved the game then, and we can save it again by following *The Unbroken Line*'s example now.

Mike Ditka
January 2010

Introduction

In 1982 pro football was very different from today. Though top players were national names, they weren't yet the bank-breaking superstars whose every move was followed by a ravenous sports media and who received million-dollar bonuses before they ever played a down. Most players were middle-class, making less than six figures a year, and salaries were rigidly and secretively controlled by teams that had complete control over players' lives, careers, and even their bodies. They had no medical benefits, no retirement plans, no say in where they played or for how long, and a miniscule share of the multibillion-dollar television contract that had been signed a year earlier. In short, NFL players in 1982 were hired, disposable muscle.

The strike that was called in 1982 had more to do with union leaders' egos and self-interested power grabs than truly gaining benefits for their members. They wanted the exclusive ability to negotiate contracts for each and every player, giving the athletes even less say in their own fates. The league and the union assumed they could play out the strike on their own timelines, and to their own satisfaction, while the players simply sat at home and waited for the verdict to be handed down from above.

Unfortunately for the league and the union, things didn't work out that way. A small cadre of players, led by a seasoned veteran and a young Dallas attorney, took matters into their own hands and took on both the NFL and the union behind closed doors ... and won. For the first time, the players themselves took control of their own fates, and the dam got its first crack—a crack that eventually broke open with the decertification of the union and the advent of free agency years later. It was a small but vital revolt in the history of the NFL, and its story has remained untold until right now. It's called *The Unbroken Line*.

Justin Ware

Justin is a Wisconsin native, Hollywood screenwriter and Green Bay Packers fanatic whose family has owned season tickets for more than seventy-five years.

The Unbroken Line

Many football aficionados can rifle off the stats of their favorite teams as if the trivia were gospel; few, however, know the history of the business side of football. Fewer still take the business into consideration in the ordinary course of fandom. Most fans follow the draft and trades, but it rarely goes past who got whom for however much. How many know, for example, what gave rise to free agency in the first place? President Truman may have gone a little too far when he said, "There is nothing new in the world except the history you do not know." But he knew that history, as the proverb has it, repeats itself. The last NFL players strike was in 1987; the one before that was in 1982. Since the beginning of 2007, the word has been spreading that another NFL players strike is inevitable.

The current leaders of the NFL Players Association will be the bargainers should a strike take place, and this is a problem. When the 1987 strike commenced, the owners were prepared; the union leaders were not. Only the owners had learned from history, and their scab team season forced the players back onto the field. The union, having failed to achieve even the most meager of players' demands, was decertified. The union leaders had failed and, simultaneously, revealed to any interested party an undeniable incompetence. Just five years earlier, in the strike of 1982, the union leaders claimed and boasted a strategic success against the owners in favor of the unionists; our story will show that these "leaders" merely had provided their signatures for the documents of that early players' rights victory. The claim that they were the final arbiters of that success is an unscrupulous one; but worse, if the claim were true, it just means they didn't even bother to learn from their own past to prevent the disastrous results in 1987. Worse, they're back. They've been rehired and are ready to serve.

Another strike seems to be looming, and it is vital to reveal the incompetence that hung like a fog over NFL business all those years ago, and which continues to hang to this day. Fans will be surprised, and many will be angered, when they learn what was going on then and how it sheds light on what is going on now. Former and current players alike will have a fiercer, more personal reaction when they learn these facts. In any case, we are glad that the truth is finally coming out and sincerely hope that our story will help to force true and honest negotiations to take place finally, for the sake of old and new players, for the fans, and for the integrity of football. This David-and-Goliath tale needs to be told because players and fans are responsible to know the game they love, and how those who helped build it have been treated over the years.

The public has a right to know the truth; the players need to know it. This story will reveal how greed and iniquity have beset professional football and how the very same NFL Players Association leaders— some former brethren of the gridiron, no less—and their acolytes have shamefully, time and again, misrepresented their unionists because of a past incompetence, a questionable resurgence, and an eventual illicit, unilateral control of assets that should have been intended for NFLPA members, retired and active. These leaders have done more than sully the very notion of good faith by their treatment of their constituents; they have managed to make themselves and their successors wealthy in the process.

Even before their base subsumption of responsibility for the 1982 victory, they acted in ways to make one question whether they have the union members on their minds at all. Take, for example, their actual attempts to squelch the existence of independent representation so that they (the union leaders) could serve as the exclusive agent for every player. Were these leaders incredibly blind to the blatant conflict of interest here (more on this later), or did they have someone else's interest at heart? Their transgressions have been many, and they continue.

In the first years of the third millennium, retired and active NFL players signed an exclusive agreement with the NFLPA and one of its subsidiaries, the marketing company Players, Inc. Under this "group licensing agreement," the organizations contracted to represent each player in the marketing of his name, image, and other personal data. In January 2007, Herb Adderley, Hall-of-Famer of the Green Bay Packers and Dallas Cowboys, and many fellow retired NFL players sued the NFLPA and Players, Inc., for breach of contract.

Adderley and his comrades alleged that the union had deliberately failed to seek or distribute royalties for the likenesses and statistics of the retired players that are featured in the "vintage" section of the top-selling Madden NFL video game by Electronic Arts (EA). The jury agreed. According to the Associated Press, one member of the ten-person jury said of their unanimous verdict: "We felt we had to send a message that the union needs to represent all its members, [and] we felt the players' union didn't do that."[1] The AP noted that the verdict was found in the light of some pretty damning evidence: Adderley's attorneys presented a letter from an NFLPA executive that directed EA to "scramble" the images of retired players lest they have to pay them.

Tony Davis and Joe DeLamielleure, former players and contemporary retirees' rights activists, had for a long time been aware of the NFLPA's dubious interpretations of their contractual arrangements with retired players. It was no surprise to Tony when he snapped open the morning paper to find that the jury had agreed with Adderley-and-company's allegations, a lot....

1   Elias, "Jury Orders NFL Union to Pay $28.1M to Retirees."

A Conference Call

February 15, 2009

Tony Davis: Hey, Joe D.

Joe DeLamielleure: Tony?

Tony: Yeah. Got caller ID?

Joe: Hey, I'm with the grandson—who has figured out how to answer the phone ...

Tony: Ah, I see. So, did you see the *USA Today* this morning? Full spread on Herb's lawsuit. Can you believe this? Here—listen to this: "Jury says union liable to players for 28.1 million dollars."

Joe: You're shittin' me. That's a damned victory, if I've ever heard one.

Tony: In a way, I guess it is. But, get this: that money comes from the union, not from the leaders, the bastards who breached their fiduciary duty to the players. So, the jury found that those freakin' guys who run the union breached their duty—and, BA-BA-DA-DA, the union pays?

Joe: Why don't the leaders pay?

Tony: They weren't individually sued. They are the union, where it counts, but not where it pays, I guess.

Joe: At least those schmucks got their comeuppance some way. And publicly. You know, over all these years, those guys, from Upshaw on, have been greasy from the start. And made themselves millionaires. It *is* a crime in itself that they don't have to pay. Shit, T. D., those scumbags get a smack to their ego, but not to their bank account ... unbelievable! Think they care? Bet they don't.... Anyway, were you playing in '82?

Tony: Yeah, it was my last year.

Joe: Remember when Garvey and Upshaw actually tried to sell us on the idea of letting them represent all of us exclusively, as agents for all our contracts? No personal lawyers or agents allowed ...

Tony: 'Course I remember that. But we all raised such a stink just as the strike was starting, that they dropped that dumbass idea from the agenda. Now, it's the same old shit: I can't tell if it's incompetence or greed or both. Just because over twenty-five years ago, they settle some strike, they get the nerve to misrepresent their players as only an incompetent can. Only difference is they were wily enough to find a way to make themselves rich by virtually having exclusive control and probable part ownership of the NFLPA marketing company.

Joe: Wait a minute, Tony. I agree with you that they are greedy sonsuhbitches, and are probably incompetent too. But let's get something straight. I know the union leaders have been claiming that '82 strike settlement, but they had little or nothing to do with it, not really. That's why what's going on now means so much, Tony.

Tony: I'm not following you.

Joe: It's pretty simple: Upshaw and company did not have anything to do with what really ended that strike in '82. I mean, they were there. And, yeah, they signed papers and stuff, because they were authorized to do so. But what really happened is that they and the owners were wedged into that position and couldn't get out. The fact that the same jerk-offs and their successors are either still in the union or still weighing influence on a player or league matters is more ridiculous than you can imagine.

Tony: Again, not sure I follow.

Joe: Man, I was the temporary player rep for the Browns back then. I was subbing for Doug Dieken, okay? Right before the strike was settled, those "leaders" sent us home. They sounded the damn retreat, I'm telling you. I was even going to my second job, ya know, screw football, the day the strike ended. No one called to tell me, "Not necessary, Joe." Then out of nowhere, out of nowhere, the strike gets settled. And the arbitrator is three thousand miles away! Now how do you settle the strike when the arbitrator is three thousand miles away? Listen, hold on for a second. It's gonna beep twice, and then I'll pick back up. I'm calling Billy Joe DuPree for a conference call—know him? We were teammates at Michigan State.

Tony: Yeah, I know him. I wanted to add him to a new lawsuit we want to file against those guys, individually. What's he know about this?

Joe: He was there. Had a hand in it. No, he had two hands in it. Let him tell ya—hold on....

CHAPTER 1
Passive Resistance

A view from Billy Joe DuPree

From 1969–73 I played tight end for Michigan State University. I'll be honest with you: when it really sank in—when I realized I was going to receive a first-rate education *and* play football with and against the best in the country—I felt proud. And when I went out onto the field for the first time as a Spartan, I felt humble. I love football. It's the greatest game in the world. The game taught loyalty, honor, and sacrifice. It proved that any team, with a continuity of effort and desire, could defeat any foe.

Back then, I should point out, the Civil Rights Act was barely five years old. In the campus courtyard, you heard students discussing recent assassinations: Martin Luther King Jr. and John and Robert Kennedy. Under that shadow, I was tabbed an All-American candidate during my junior year, and I was "on the picks" of several professional football scouting wires. Old men with big smiles told me that I would be a first-round choice in the next year's professional football league draft, but I knew I wasn't just a football player. I prided myself on being an articulate, intelligent, and devoted man to God, my family, my teammates, and my principles. I can tell you the moment I defined those principles to myself.... I must have had them all along because my mother raised me well—but I had never said, *Billy Joe, this is what you stand for....*

During the Big Ten basketball season of 1971–72, I was involved in an on-campus political struggle. A small team of students and athletes took action against prejudice and racism. This event prepared me for what I would undergo in a similar crusade as a professional player just a few years down the line.

Sam Riddle was a political science major and campus activist. He quickly ran up the stairs that led from the lobby to the second floor of the Men's Athletic Dorm, shouting, "Billy Joe? You up here? Come on, man. We're gonna be late!" His anxiety was genuine—and typical. I leaned my head out of the bathroom door of my dorm room and said, quietly and calmly, "Relax."

"Come on, B. J. You do this just to mess with me."

"We have plenty of time, Sam. Everyone's ready. Anyway, if I'm going to be in front of such a huge crowd without my football helmet on, I certainly want to look my best, don't I, Sam? They say the man makes the clothes, but I'm not sure."

"You're a pain in the ass. You look fine. Please, brother—hurry up, we're definitely *late*. I can't believe that you just got out of the shower!"

His frustration turned to laughter after I stared quizzically at his reflection, and then returned attention to my hair. Though I once had a reputation for having a disregard for punctuality, he had come to realize that I actually had timing. He did not know that in a few moments, the both of us were going to walk past people who keep people out. He didn't know they would allow us to walk right past them, right under the Spartan boards as our team warmed up with layups and fifteen-footers.

Sam and I left Spartan Hall just before tip-off. As we approached the arena, we were met by an army of students, student-athletes, and some political science majors. Our group had planned to voice a protest against the Big Ten Athletic Conference: apparently the Conference felt that black referees shouldn't call Big Ten basketball games. They had not given any legitimate explanation for not hiring qualified black officials and knew they couldn't give one. So they said nothing, and their indifference reeked of prejudice.

"Come on," I said to the crowd that had huddled in the parking lot. "Let's go inside. We can stand outside of this arena all day and accomplish just a little. Maybe make it into the school paper ... third page. Or we can go inside and make a statement. Something people can't ignore."

Sam said, "What the hell are you talking about?"

"We are going to go inside the arena and walk right onto the gym floor. The entire group. No one is going to mess with us: who's going to mess with their fellow athletes, especially in front of ten thousand admiring fans, for merely taking a philosophical position? We'll walk on that floor and passively—yet strongly—state our feelings. We will make a difference because there are too many people out there who know we're right."

"You sure they won't do anything?"

"Sam, again, what are they going to do? Are they going to arrest some of the players who are scheduled to play in the same game the people are there to watch? I don't think so. And if they do, so what, we go to jail. We get bail, and we go to the papers, telling them that we were there to interrupt their entertainment, for a moment, to expose a moral wrong, an injustice in practice right before their eyes. *People will be on our side.*"

"You know, the more you talk, the more convinced I become. Maybe you should major in political science," Sam said.

As we entered the arena, I gathered everyone together and said, "We will all walk on the floor as a unit, join hands, and do nothing else—no words. When the time presents itself, we will leave. Trust me, we will know when that time is. Whatever you do, do not give anyone any excuse to create an adversarial situation. Close your ears to comments and your hearts to anger. If we handle this matter appropriately, we will succeed, okay? Everyone understand and agree?"

Everyone in the group quietly responded, "Yes."

With that we headed down to the playing floor approximately five minutes before the tip-off. The security guards and school officials recognized who we were; no one tried to stop us. We took a route toward the scorer's table and then took approximately ten steps onto the hardwood … and stood there. The players who were taking layups immediately ceased. A few balls bounced, and then the sound of the crowd faded. Some players held basketballs in their hands; others put them back in the ball racks and headed to stand near us. For one full minute, we all stood on the court. And then got a response none of us expected: everyone in the arena rose in support. There was a loud silence, a wordless message, sent throughout the state of Michigan and the rest of the Big Ten. After the crowd stood silently for about thirty seconds, the fans started to applaud and cheer; and we, students in street clothes and athletes in basketball uniforms, applauded them. The following week, the Big Ten commissioner assigned some black officials to referee Big Ten basketball.

This was an important moment in my life, and as I mentioned before, it prepared me for another major challenge, one involving my family and livelihood. People today are oblivious to the truth of what really happened in professional football when I played. Professional football was not about luxury and three-million-dollar Super Bowl commercials. We had our share of playboys and exhibitionists, but professional sports was just economically different then ... for the players, anyway. We had low salaries, virtually no medical or health benefits, and a union (the NFLPA) that wanted to get rid of individual representation so that they, the union, could negotiate our contracts and effectively control (along with the owners) our lives. I knew things had to change, and on July 11, 1982, I knew I'd found the person who could make that happen.

Tony: So, who is this guy?

Joe: The judge?

Tony: The guy you said you found. How'd you find him?

Billy Joe: I saw an article that he wrote for the *Dallas Morning News*. He was pretty famous around the locker room by that time, anyway. The Cowboys, Landry, they all respected him. Got a bunch of people off a bunch o' stuff.

Joe: He had a lot of Cowboys as clients then.

Tony: He was an agent?

Joe: No, he's a lawyer. Was a judge for a while after all this went down.

Tony: Well, why him specifically?

Billy Joe: He knew what he was talking about in that article. And when we met on that golf course, I could tell he was one of us....

CHAPTER 2
Good-bye, Big Apple—Hello, Big D

A view from Spencer Kopf

One side of the stands at Upsala College in New Jersey was full of young campers between the ages of ten and fifteen. The counselors' championship game of the Walt Frazier Summer Basketball Camp was winding down. One team was led by Captain Walt "Clyde" Frazier, Hall of Fame guard of the New York Knicks and still *the* true fan favorite of the City of New York. In game seven of the 1970 NBA Championship, Walt nearly single-handedly dismantled a great Los Angeles Lakers team. And he would do it again in 1973. The press gave Walt the sobriquet "Clyde"—after the dapper bank robber Clyde Barrow—for his stylish dress and talent of stealing the basketball from even the best ball handlers in the league.

I first met Clyde through George Kalinsky, the renowned photographer for Madison Square Garden. George lived across the street from my home on Long Island. He has been a mentor to me since childhood. More than any person, George believed in me and made me feel the confidence and courage to seek and achieve any goal and face any situation head on, in sports or in life. He was responsible for my getting the jobs with Clyde's management company and basketball summer camps.

The former backup center of the New York Knicks, Luther Rackley, two college players, and I rounded out Walt's squad. The other team's captain was Dean "The Dream" Meminger, backup guard of the New York Knicks and former NCAA champion with Marquette University. His center for the day was Nate Bowman, backup center of the New York Knicks. Three college players completed the Dream's team.

Noel Brown was a former college football player and assistant coach at Texas Southern University. He was a counselor at the camp and as close a friend to Clyde as I was. Noel had helped in recruiting high school players for his university, and he coached the offensive line. The student body at his school referred to him as "The Big Groove" for his being the coolest and toughest guy on campus. But despite his Goliath stature, he had (and still has) a very engaging, warm personality. In fact, he was considered to be a big teddy bear with the campers; they all loved him. He would later work for Irwin Weiner, Clyde's agent, for a brief time; and he would join my office in Dallas in early 1980 after I decided to pursue my interest in sports representation. Noel also later became my bailiff in the municipal court. Most importantly, he has been a devoted friend throughout the years. He was sitting on Clyde's bench that day and reminisced the following.

In the middle of the second half, Clyde passed to Spence five feet outside the top of the key and yelled, "Drill it." Spence put up a one-hand set shot and scorched the cords from twenty-four feet. No rim. I mean nothing but the bottom of the net. It was Clyde

67, Dream 59. The next time down the floor, Luther blocked the shot of a player heading down the three-second lane that goes clear to mid-court. And Spence is breaking with the ball, pushing it up in front of him. This guy ran up to block his drive to the bucket, and Spence hit Clyde with a behind-the-back pass, in stride. Clyde laid it off the glass. It was sweet. See, Spence was playing in what players call the Zone. And Clyde knew it. So he kept feeding him the ball. Both Spence and Clyde had thirty-something points that game. They won going away. No contest.

When the clock finally ran out, the teams shook hands and headed to greet the kids. As I approached the bench, Noel handed me a towel and said, "Great game, little buddy. Way to shoot the rock."

Wiping my face, I wheezed through the towel, "Groove, they were doubling up on Clyde. I was left wide open."

"So? You still had to hit the shots, and they were all long-range. Plus, Marques[2] sure taught you how to handle the ball. It sure was pretty watching you move up and down the floor. Just listen to those kids. You even blew away Clyde. He loved it. He was smiling big the whole time."

Clyde stylishly strolled over and sat down next to us. The campers were flying around seeking autographs from the players and getting pictures taken with whomever they could. Over the commotion, Clyde said, "Little Buddy, you sure were tearin' it up. I didn't realize you could fill it up like that. That's as good as I've seen in a long time. No joke."

"Not so bad yourself, Clyde. Look at the stat sheet. You had sixteen assists and all those points."

---

2   Marques Haynes, Harlem Globetrotter and arguably the finest ball handler of all time.

As we continued to talk about the game, the kids headed out of the gym, and all the players shuffled languidly to the locker room. Five-on-five for nearly two hours with no substitutions left even the pros exhausted. After changing, we all headed for the parking lot to go home. Clyde peered over his car and said, "Let's grab a bite at the Deli, Wednesday." *The Famous Deli* at 39th and Lexington had the best corned-beef sandwich on rye in the city.

I arrived at the restaurant to find Clyde already sitting at his favorite table. I sat down, and we ordered lunch. As the waitress was leaving the table, Clyde unrolled his napkin, meticulously arranged his silverware, and said, "Look, Spence, I know that Irwin relied on you to help him with all those football contracts. And he'd never admit it himself, but Irwin can't talk to players like you can, 'cause you're one of us. For guys like us, it's about the game, you know. When you go to Dallas, there is no reason why you can't do the same thing there. The other day when we were playing head-to-head with Dream, it didn't intimidate you one bit. And you're that way off the court, too. What I'm saying is, no one knew much about *me* until the Salukis won the NIT. But after that game, after all those New Yorkers saw me, the Knicks had to take me. The same can be for you. When you get to Dallas, don't wait on the sidelines for something to happen, make it happen. You got to take it yourself, just like you did here. You do that. You'll see I'm right."

"Thanks, Clyde. Thanks for everything," I said.

He had already bitten into his sandwich, so he simply nodded and chewed. "Of course ..."

For some reason, that corned-beef sandwich was better than usual that day.

That Friday I left for Texas. I reached the Kappa Sigma house at SMU on Sunday evening. Upon my arrival, Alumni Advisor Jack Haaker warmly greeted me. He had arranged for me to stay at the house, rent free, until I secured a job. I would be taking a review course in preparation for the bar exam that November, so the accommodation was extremely generous. I had four months to devote every minute I spent awake to study the laws of Texas.

My southern friends really became my family. I had been a New York City kid but was lucky enough to have been raised mostly on Long Island. By the time I reached college age, a scholarship to Oklahoma City University pretty much guaranteed that I would cross the Mason-Dixon Line for a while and get my education and play some ball in the South. I was one scared Yankee. But it turned out I would meet some of the best people I had ever known in Oklahoma and Texas.

People say the bar exam is tough. People are right. Let's put it this way: in Texas, even if you know that as a lawyer the closest you will ever get to the oil industry is when you fill your car at the corner station, you still have to be prepared for the Oil and Gas section of the bar exam, whether or not you ever studied the subject in law school. As it happens, I took a decent bar review course and passed the exam without developing an ulcer. Then I got an Assistant City Attorney's position at the Dallas City Attorney Prosecutor's Office. I remained at the fraternity house, paid the forgiven rent, and assisted the actives as my services were needed. I will submit a slight admission: I suited up, pretending to be an undergraduate, to quarterback the chapter's flag football team to the semifinals of the interfraternity intramural flag football championship. We took to the field to the theme music from the movie *Patton*. They were a great group, and as corny as it may be, it was a very special time in my life.

I finally had to move out, grow up, and get an apartment. But I would still find myself hanging with Jack over at the frat house. From time to time, we were joined in the game room by another fellow alumnus of that chapter, Lamar Hunt. Jack was unaware that Lamar and I had met, so he reintroduced us one afternoon. We both politely interrupted and informed Jack that we had originally met each other back in 1975 while I was traveling under the employ of W. F. Sports. I explained that I was working for the company of the sports agent that represented Walter White, the fourth-round draft pick of the professional football team that Mr. Hunt happened to own. Lamar would become one of the most prominent owners in NFL history. He owned the Dallas Texans of the AFL, which would become the Kansas City Chiefs, and he was responsible for the negotiations between the NFL and AFL. The trophy for the AFC championship is called the Lamar Hunt Trophy for innumerable reasons. The man even coined the term Super Bowl! Guys like Jack and Lamar were the type of men who molded me as a young adult into the man I am today.

As my work increased, my free time decreased. I was competing in local basketball, soccer, and softball leagues, and dating; my time was occupied. But the three of us, along with other alumni from that chapter, would run into each other at local chapter events, national chapter events, or at the house. When I did get to see the alumni, it felt like no time had passed. I still feel that way about them to this very day.

Tony: Kappa Sig, huh?

Billy Joe: Yeah, he's a real frat boy—I mean devoted ... And in a way, that's what got this done for us—

Joe: Yeah, this is weird, though …

Billy Joe: Yeah, if Spence hadn't been in that fraternity … Hell, even if he had been but was a scumbag and no one respected him, the thing we pulled off back in '82 probably wouldn't have worked out at all. It turned out that we saw eye to eye about—about ethical questions, you know? And he credits the same mentors you or I would: his college coaches and his fraternity brothers, and he's just not full of shit like agents are. I mean, he pulled some *crazy* things, Tony, believe me; but, like I say, if the Judge likes you, he'll protect you like a Rottweiler.

Tony: What kind of *crazy* things?

CHAPTER 3
Meet Fred Dean

A view from Spencer Kopf

I walked down to the conference room that Noel was using as a temporary office since he had arrived from the city via Houston. He left W. F. Sports that late summer and came down to work with me on a part time basis. I rolled around the doorjamb and tossed the new *Street and Smith* sports magazine onto the long table. It slid under his waiting palm, and he looked up at me, arching his eyebrows, as he shouldered his phone.

I said quietly, "Groove, check out this *Street and Smith*. It deals with the current professional football rosters."

He nodded seriously and went back to the phone call. It turns out I had found him in deep conversation with Fred Dean, one of his former players that he had coached and trained at Texas Southern. A few minutes later, Noel knocked on my door and asked to speak with me as soon as possible. I sensed an urgency and solemn tone in his voice. The big fella seemed quite worried and distraught.

"Chief," Noel began, "do you remember the player from TSU that you helped get in that Bowl game for seniors, when you were at W. F.?"

"That's the guy we took to Manny Wolfe's for dinner, right? Then you, Clyde, Ed, and I went to the john to wash up after we ordered a plate of appetizers for eight. When we returned, we found our friend from TSU licking his fingers with the empty platter in front of him. This is the same guy, who, after you had taken him to pick out a new suit for his press conference, showed up the next day in a brand-new charcoal suit ... with the sleeves of the jacket cut off at the elbow, exposing the sleeves of the shiniest purple shirt I've ever seen. On his head, he was brandishing a royal purple derby, complete with a chicken's tail feather dyed purple to match. Do you recall the prissy shriek Irwin let out? That scream shook the entire high-rise."

Having laughed hysterically throughout my description, Noel responded, "That's him. Do you remember how good he was as a player?"

"Yeah," I said. "He was good. If I recall correctly, he went early in the second round."

"You think you can work your magic again? Fred Dean, the best offensive lineman I ever coached, just got cut from the Bears. He is a better player than that big guy was, easy. He has played tight end, guard, and tackle. He's a player. He was with Miami for most of the preseason last year and got released. The Bears picked him up this season and just released him. Will you help him?"

"Well, let me look at the alternative. If I don't help him, you'll mope around the office all football season. We certainly can't have that, can we?"

"Thanks. It means a lot to me. Fred is a great player with a great work ethic. If given a fair chance, he'll make it."

"Hey, he doesn't have to be great to play the offensive line. He has to be quicker than the guy across from him and have good technique to overcome any lack in size and strength. You said he played tight end? Well, that means that he is probably quicker than most defensive linemen. This means, Coach, if you taught him proper technique, he will have a decent shot. Groove, relax. Your buddy made it through the entire preseason before getting released. That means, kemo sabe, if we find him the right situation, he'll be fine. So let's get Fred on the next flight to Dallas. How's that?"

"Spence, that's great. Thanks, man."

"After you deal with Fred to get him in here, make yourself useful and contact our buddy and get the most up-to-date injury report for each roster in the league."

"Right on, Spence," he said as he snatched up the phone and rewedged it between his ear and shoulder.

I arrived at the office after the morning docket call at the Dallas County Courthouse to find Noel and Fred visiting in the small conference room. Fred Dean was six-foot-four, 265 pounds; he had a very athletic build for an offensive lineman. The scouting report on Fred was flattering, yet brief. His attributes were his quickness, speed, and excellent agility. He was very versatile, which proved to be an extremely valuable selling point. The only drawback that the scouting report emphasized was the college football schedule that he had played had not been against marquee division-one schools. After going through all the pleasantries and sharing some war stories, we got right down to it.

"When you were down in Miami, how did you think you were doing?" I asked.

"Fine. I thought I was having an excellent camp. I felt strong and quick. I was shocked I got released. In fact, one of the guys in the front office, Dick Meyers, told me that he didn't want them to release me. He was a real nice guy. He said I did everything they asked of me and more. I played several positions—I guess that was impressive, but to be honest with you, that made it hard for me to settle in on technique. Maybe I should have concentrated on one position. But that's what they had me do. It wasn't a fair test, but I thought I made the most of it."

"Okay. What happened in Chicago?"

"Nothin' really. They never really gave me a shot to do anything. I was pretty much gone almost as soon as I arrived. I didn't understand why they brought me in if they weren't even going to really look at what I could do, you know?"

"Look, Fred, I can't promise you anything. But if your question is if I think I can get you placed, the answer is yes. Do I know how soon and with what team? No. But let's put it this way: you have some serious skills, which makes you a very interesting commodity. In my opinion, I'm shocked you were released; you have extreme versatility in your game. So, here is what we are going to do. First, the three of us are going to go out for lunch and have a great meal. Second, you are going to head home to Gainesville, stay in playing shape as if you are in camp, and check in with me at least once a day. Third, when I tell you to go somewhere, you got to do it, no questions asked. Deal?"

"Deal."

I asked, "Fred, do you like steak?"

"Yes, sir," he said enthusiastically.

"Big Groove, does Fred like the sight of many attractive women?"

Noel laughed a shy laugh—shy for him, anyway, because it shook the room. He had anticipated what was coming.

"Fred, why don't you and Noel go down to the second floor? I'll arrange for a table, and I'll meet you down there in, let's say, twenty minutes. Now, both you guys get out of here before I change my mind and send you both to McDonalds."

Fred said, "Groove, what's on the second floor?"

Noel started giggling and squeezed out, "You're about to be blown away."

"Fred," I added, "Noel means that literally." Noel lost it, cracking up in only the way he could. Finally, as they approached the door to leave the office, Noel leaned over to Fred and whispered to him like two young kids keeping a secret from the teacher. Fred bellowed out, "Playboy Club ... bullshit! No. Really?"

As they opened the door, I yelled, "I'll get a table so Fred can meet Ruby."

Both Noel and Fred started laughing and joking; as they left the office, they were grinning from ear to ear. After leaving Chicago unhappy and uncertain about his football career, Fred Dean, in that brief morning, had a revitalized purpose and confidence, which is where his thoughts needed to be. Noel and I both knew that once he got placed, Fred Dean would make it happen. Obviously, he proved us right, in a big, Super Bowl-champion way.

The following Monday

I sat in my office reviewing the injury report from the weekend games and noticed that Washington Redskin offensive guard Ron Saul went down with a knee injury that was certain to lay him up. I immediately called a contact of mine to retrieve as much information regarding the status of that player and the extent of his injury. Another Redskin offensive lineman had also reaggravated a previous knee injury and might be questionable for the next game or, worse, for a few. More importantly, the new assistant general manager of the Redskins, by what must have been some alignment of the stars, just happened to be Dick Meyers, that fellow from Miami who had wanted to keep Fred on the Dolphin roster. The question was how we would play this round of cards, and win, without a showdown. I checked the rest of the league's injury reports with a similar situation as Washington and called Noel into the office.

"Noel, make reservations on the first available flight for Fred to New Orleans tomorrow. Then put me on a flight arriving near or around the same time. Tell him I'll meet him at the lobby of the airport hotel. Then call our buddy in Reston and have him tell Guback that he heard Fred and I would be in the Crescent City tomorrow. Let me know when all of that's done."

Guback was the Redskins' beat writer for the *Washington Star*. In fact, he had written favorably about the way I had handled the renegotiation of the contract for my first football client, Danny "Lightning" Buggs, who was currently practicing in Reston with the Skins. Danny wound up getting more money than the All-Pro receiver Drew Pearson of the Dallas Cowboys. That result brought other players to my door. Now I figured Mr. Guback would be interested in Fred's story, especially if Danny delivered the news.

"Got it," Noel replied.

I attempted to buzz Hazel (Hazel Fretz of the executive suite) but received no reply—so I half-yelled her name from my desk.

Hazel came strolling in about fifteen seconds later and, with a half smirk—and with a joking tone resembling Jonathan Winters— responded, "Yeeeessss."

I chuckled for a second and then said, "Very cute. Okay, here is what I need for you to do...."

She grinned a foolish, wide grin and arched her eyebrows.... She had gotten comfortable with me since I moved into her executive suites, and was already yanking my chain.

"Stop. I'm trying to focus," I continued. "How do you expect me to deal with this stuff if you keep cracking me up?"

"Because it's fun, silly," she said.

"Come on, please. This is real important," I insisted, half chuckling. "Cancel my schedule for the next two days as graciously as you can. You might get some calls from the press. If any reporters call and they ask where I am, this one time you can volunteer that I am meeting a new client, Fred Dean, out of town. Just make it sound matter-of-fact. Do not put any emphasis on it. If they then ask what city, you are to respond, 'I really shouldn't have told you what I told you. So I'll just take a message, and I'll have him call you when he returns.' Something like that, okay?"

Hazel, now in a perfect imitation of Eve Arden of *Our Miss Brooks* fame, said, "I think I can handle that."

"You know, you're a mess ... you know that?" I asked.

"Absolutely," she quipped as she strolled away from the doorframe.

I quickly turned my concentration to Noel. "Groove, when is my flight and when do I arrive in New Orleans?"

"You leave at 8:10 a.m. and arrive at 10:30 a.m. Fred gets in at 10:00 a.m."

"Great. That will work out just fine. Now, call Fred and tell him to tell Nettie Belle[3] that if anyone calls for him, she is to say that Fred

---

3   Fred's mother. She was the boss.

and his attorney went out of town on business. If they ask where Fred went, tell her to say that she doesn't know. Got it?"

"Got it, Chief."

"Great. Remember, follow up with her tomorrow morning," I added. "Since we have that project under control, I am going to get back to my cases scheduled for next week in case this matter with Fred drags out a bit. And, Noel, could you also please ask Don to join me and bring his notepad? Thanks, buddy."

The next morning—The Big Easy makes it easier

I landed at the airport in New Orleans at approximately 10:45 a.m. and arrived at the hotel lobby at precisely 11:00 a.m. Sitting on a couch near the front entrance, as instructed, was the man of the hour. Fred appeared nervous and anxious to find out why he was there. He greeted me with a fretful "What's up?"

"Patience, my man. Good things come to those who wait. I am going to check you into a room, and we'll order room service for lunch. Do you know how to play gin?" Fred shook his head and looked even more confused. "Good, I'll teach you, and we'll talk about life, football, and then why we're here."

I approached the front desk, paid cash for Fred's reservation, and strolled down to his room. As we went in, Fred said, "Come on, Spence, why are we here?"

"First things first. Call room service and order me a cheeseburger with nothing on it, medium rare, and make the fries crispy. I'll have a Pepsi. Then order what you want. Then we'll talk about why we are here."

Fred ordered room service. He had to send back the order two times before the kitchen got it right. He'd given me a hairy stare when he'd sent away two chicken dishes for the second time. Fred, already anxious, was becoming frustrated at the food, at the kitchen…. "What are we doing here, Spence?"

"Look, Fred. Let me make something perfectly clear to you. Noel loves you like a little brother, and I can see why. You contracted with me to help get you back in the league. I am laying out my bread and my time to create a scenario that may cut short your wait. This trip may prevent you from sitting at home with your thumb up your ass waiting for the phone to ring. Now, I think what we have going on here has a genuinely decent shot to work if the Redskins have not been stocking away some backup offensive lineman somewhere. So, let things play out and calm the fuck down. Besides, I promised your momma I would take care of you and help you get your dream back. Believe it when I say that, after talking with Noel about what a lady your mother is, there is no way in the world I am about to disappoint her. So lighten up and let me do my thing, okay?" Fred nodded in agreement. "Okay. Now, let me call the office and check in. Then I'll teach you some gin until the food arrives. When the food arrives, I'll fill you in on everything, and we'll talk about football, women, or whatever. Now shuffle the cards and deal eleven to me and ten to you."

"All right—cool," Fred agreed as he shrugged and began shuffling the pasteboards sloppily on the bed.

As our meal arrived, Fred was already down five bucks at a penny a point. Then, right in the middle of our lunch, Hazel called to tell me that Steve Guback of the *Washington Star* had called regarding Fred Dean; and that forty-five minutes later, Dick Meyers of the Washington Redskins had called, asking for me to call him back as soon as possible. I instructed Hazel to call Mr. Meyers's secretary, not Mr. Meyers, and leave the telephone number of the hotel and the room extension. Thirty minutes later, a sudden ring filled the room. I quickly knocked with three points and snapped up the phone. "Hello."

"Hello, Spencer, Dick Meyers of the Washington Redskins. Thanks for calling back."

"No problem. I'm just sittin' around. How can I help?"

"Well, I'll get straight to the point. I understand you are representing Fred Dean now, correct?"

"That is accurate," I replied.

"Is Fred with you in New Orleans?"

"Yes, he's right here. We were about to head out for a meeting, why?"

"Well, Fred knows me really well, and I have a situation here in Washington that would really benefit Fred's career."

I sheepishly complimented him by saying, "Fred shared everything about his stay in Miami and Chicago with me. He thinks very highly of you, despite being released by Miami. He was very disappointed. They had him playing several positions, so he couldn't settle in at one job to prove his worth."

Dick responded, "Ask Fred. I told them that they shouldn't release him—that he was valuable because he could play several positions and could easily fill in for injured players because of his versatility. That keeping him was important because you never know who is going to go down."

"That's true."

"As I said, we have circumstances here that fit Fred's situation perfectly. Ron Saul, our left offensive guard, has gone down with a season-ending injury, and another one of our linemen is nicked up pretty bad. Fred could fill in or even start at one of those positions. Our offensive scheme is similar to Miami's, and Fred would be able to pick it up easy. Also, I'm here, and I've been selling getting Fred in here to the coaches and Bobby Beathard since I joined the Skins' staff."

"We're listening."

"Bobby said he knows you from the Danny Buggs contract. He said you seem to care about 'the player.' He said that you flew up to Carlisle after having an emergency appendectomy with a rope tied around your waist so that Danny wouldn't sign his contract without your guidance."

"That's all true. So, what's your point?"

"My point is, Fred belongs here with the Redskins. It's a perfect fit. Plus, once again, I'm here, and he knows I think a lot of him. I love his versatility and his work ethic. You never hear him make an excuse, and he never complains. We got along in Miami, and it will be even better here. So, let's try to work something out to get Fred up here."

"Well, I—"

"Look, I realize you are in New Orleans.... But this is a better fit up here for Fred. Plus I won't let him down. I'm here, and I have the authority to sign him."

"Fred has heard every word of this conversation. What are you proposing besides a sizable roster bonus and decent signing bonus?" I asked.

We hashed the numbers back and forth, and Dick grew more comfortable with me and I with him. I could see why Fred liked him. It *was* a perfect fit ... why else would we fly to New Orleans? Well, the gumbo's damn good.

Back to Dallas

Fred and I arrived in Dallas from New Orleans early that evening. We drove from the office to the Ramada Inn next door, dropped off Fred's luggage, and checked him in. He was to leave for Washington the following morning. Noel greeted us in the lobby, gushing with pride. He and Fred were pumped up, high with joy, and they would be that way all night. As we left the hotel to walk next door to the second floor for dinner, the two big guys, walking on either side of me, suddenly picked me up off the ground by my armpits and carried me between them all the way to the entrance of the Playboy Club. It was their night ... how could I complain?

CHAPTER 4
Leadership and Brotherhood

A view from Spencer Kopf, August 1980

The executive director of the fraternity, Richard Huebner, welcomed all the young brothers to the Leadership Conference, and just as he was about to introduce me as the keynote speaker, the hysterical comedian Professor Irwin Corey bounded upon the stage. He politely excused himself and took over the microphone. Professor Corey was garbed in an oversize tuxedo with tails that had never been pressed, a white shirt, string tie, black-with-white-trim U.S. Keds sneakers, and hair so disheveled that it looked like it had never been washed, brushed, or combed. The professor proceeded to lay them in the aisle. And this was a mere precursor to a show that all the brothers would attend at the Playboy Club Showroom later that night. After winding up his short teaser routine, the professor added something to this effect:

I believe I was responsible to introduce the keynote speaker of this conference. Now, I have been told that your speaker could have been a United States Senator, the owner of a professional football team, or the first man on the moon. Unfortunately, you guys have to settle for the former chief persecutor of traffic tickets. And now, since I forget his name, I am just going to leave and tell you I look forward to seeing your drooling faces next door after his speech.

The conference stood, applauded, and cheered the professor as he exited the room ... with a Playboy bunny on each arm.

The executive director retook control of the microphone and handsomely introduced me. I then proceeded with a speech on leadership and brotherhood, topics that had been assigned. The speech expressed my thoughts on leadership within a fraternity and a student body, and how my relationships within our fraternity had assisted me; I explained how Kappa Sigma had molded me as a student and as a man in my everyday life. I wrapped up the speech as follows:

One of the symbols of our brotherhood is our keeping of small, nonetheless important, secrets. There's a simple, choreographed handshake that represents a promise to others, who, just like you, made a bond that transcends friendship ... and can you believe it? Think for a moment. Think that this can mean that when you cross the country, or even the sea, you can through a simple handshake know that you have brothers you've never met. We also carry with us the letters below our crest—all but Greek to anyone else—but significant bits we literally take to the grave. I will address each letter now. Each letter, not as it is recorded in our tradition, but as it is defined in my private thoughts—what they have come to mean to me.

Now before you roll your eyes back and say to the guy next to you, "Do you believe this guy and his cornfield?" ask yourself why you're here. No one made you stay. You're here on your own. There is no destiny—there is no plan. You are responsible for your actions, and you are here tonight. And you are here for reasons that you might not say aloud as I am now, but reasons you think about every once in awhile. Guess what? It is that way forever, guys—that is the point. It couldn't be more poetically simple: you each have people whom you can count on forever, simply because they know they can count on you.

    The first letter, as you all know, is Alpha. That letter stands for "Action." In life, you must contribute to society and to your fellow man with assurance and confidence. Always take action with thought and discretion, but take action. Do your best to see it through, so that people will know they can rely on you and your word. The next letter is Epsilon. That letter stands for "Enthusiasm." When you take on opportunities or responsibilities in your life, do it with zeal. If you want something, you have to take it. But never let your enthusiasm cloud your judgment—a little enthusiasm and plenty of responsible foresight are a potent combination. The next letter is Kappa. That letter for me stands for "Knowledge." For without knowledge, you are weak. Read and read and read some more—you have the collected efforts of humanity at your fingertips. It takes knowing some of those efforts to change even the smallest bit of the world. But not all knowledge is found in books. You have to think critically about the things you observe every day and take nothing for granted. The next letter is Delta, the letter for "Discipline." You must be disciplined in your life. Be disciplined and follow your principles, your morals, your work, your family, your beliefs, your ethics, your country, the law, your fraternity ... be disciplined in everything that is important to you. The last letter is Beta, for "Bravery." We all must have courage at different moments in our lives, despite the odds and despite the opponent; you must dig deep—find that courage to stand up for what is right, regardless of the outcome. Do that, and you will be able to look in the mirror every single day of your lives and be proud of what you see. Thank you and good-night, brothers. A-E-K-D-B.

At a later gathering of the brotherhood, I was approached by Jack Haaker, Alumni Advisor for the chapter at Southern Methodist University, host chapter for the 1980 Leadership Conference. Jack, who you will recall had arranged for me to live at the SMU house when I first moved to Dallas, greeted me and then turned to his right to introduce one of the most recognized and prominent local alumni—one who needed no introduction: Lamar Hunt, who stood at Jack's shoulder.

"Spence, you remember this guy, don't you?" Jack asked, slightly laughing. "The last time the three of us were together, we were watching TV at the house."

I politely interjected, directing my attention to our brother, saying, "It is a pleasure to see you again, sir. I thought you would be at camp. How does your football team look this year?"

"Well, we just made a few really good draft picks; I think we'll compete well," Lamar said. "By the way, Jack gave me the highlights of what was apparently quite a motivating speech you gave at the leadership conference. Senator Tower would be very proud."

"Thank you, sir. Jack may be a little prejudiced. He has been the epitome of brotherhood since I arrived in Dallas four years ago."

"I know how you feel. Jack is quite a guy. But don't tell him; he's hard enough to deal with, and we don't need him getting a big head. Our group is full of good guys, believe me. Anyway, it's always good to see you, Spence." He had been tapped on the shoulder. Lamar nodded good-bye to Jack and me and disappeared into the crowd.

CHAPTER 5
Significant Matters

A view from Spencer Kopf, Summer 1980

I had just moved up to the tenth floor of the Expressway Tower with my buddy Don Wilmarth. The Associate Municipal Judge, Gordon MacDowell, had introduced me to Don in 1977. Don was a brilliant attorney four years my senior. He was born in Dallas and had attended Jesuit High School and later Southern Methodist University for college and law school. He was as articulate then as he is today, extremely well-read, quiet-mannered, and a master of subtle humor and irony. He possessed the knowledge of more weird, variant information than anyone I have ever known. And I have found no one more trustworthy or compassionate; it is difficult to imagine a better confidant. While his physical presence is unimposing, he has an exceptional ability to chop an opposing attorney down to size with his piercing delivery of uncannily precise knowledge of the law. Don, however, first attempts to seek an amicable resolution to a conflict before resorting to the presentation of what would always seem to be an unanswerable demolition of another attorney's legal theory or tack. It is a true pleasure to watch him work and—like the boys of Monty Python—I find myself asking Don for an argument just for my own enjoyment.

I had a different approach to the law than Don. I'm forced to attribute it to a temperament molded in the Northeast. In New York, people notoriously talk faster and with what some have euphemistically called an "unpleasant directness." I had, however, figured out that one can ask "Where's the Lincoln Tunnel?" with intense demand and vehemence even if one doesn't precede the question with "Hey, Asshole." Still, the New Yorker in me would never allow a potential adversary to think, even for one moment, that our office was concerned about or intimidated by status in the industry, power, wealth, or even physical size. As a team, Don and I simply refused the possibility of coming in second. Our polarity made for a good combination; we meshed very well as fellow lawyers and as friends. My competitive juices as an athlete transferred to my profession as an attorney and sports representative. And Don's stoicism made it impossible to know where he and I were coming from or where we would take you. We had a way of putting opposing counsel—even the grittiest, most hard-nosed attorneys—at ease and discomfort at the same time.

After serving in the office of the Dallas City Attorney, I briefly practiced privately in an executive suite and then later in the office of some other young attorneys. I chose to move to the tenth floor, away from the crowded space of lawyers I worked around—not with. I offered the extra office space in the new suite to Don. He accepted, and it was great. Don handled legal matters that I didn't, and I handled those that he didn't, and we frequently employed each other's expertise.

We interviewed for a secretarial position, which we filled with Lisa Litchfield. Lisa was an extremely bright girl from upstate New York in her early twenties. She was attractive and engaging. Though she was very inexperienced, Lisa was a quick study and had excellent natural communication skills. She had a pleasant easygoing demeanor, and she quickly overcame the meekness she had on the first days in the office. Soon, the hustle of the law office was a breeze for her. But more importantly, the few players we then represented, and the many we would come to represent, grew to trust Lisa and care about her. She was someone they could confide in just as they could in me. Her presence created a familial atmosphere that contributed immensely to the early success of our office.

The previous year, before sharing an office with Don, I had represented Dallas Cowboy linebacker Michael Hegman. While Michael was in the midst of a divorce, his roommate had accused him of twenty-seven counts of forgery. The case was before Criminal District Judge Richard Mays. (Coincidentally, this would not be the only Cowboy to sit in front of Judge Mays. "Bullet" Bob Hayes, the Olympic gold medalist, world's fastest human and underrated Dallas Cowboy, had to face the judge on charges of drug delivery.) With the guidance and assistance of James A. Rolfe, who would later be the United States Attorney for the Northern District of Texas, twenty-six of the twenty-seven counts against Hegman were dismissed. The court record reflects that Mike pled no contest to one count of theft for a plea agreement of two years deferred adjudication probation. Mike met the terms of what was required of him, and the case against him was dismissed upon his release from probation.

This and other legal successes for other athletes brought our office recognition by the sports representation industry, legal community, and the Dallas Cowboys' hierarchy. Tom Landry and I were on a first-name basis: he called me Spence, and I called him Coach. Even Tex afforded me the same courtesy. Attorney-client privilege restricts what I record here, but our office soon had successfully handled other matters regarding athletes that were never leaked to the press.

After attending my fraternity's leadership conference, I had planned to assist Lisa and Don in expanding and upgrading our new digs. I arrived at the office the morning of September 10, 1980, with a copy of a newly amended draft of player incentive bonus clauses I had conjured up for the next contract negotiation.

Lisa buzzed me and said I had a large item in the mail from Charlottesville, Virginia. She was still a fairly new employee, and the package just looked important, so she had left it sealed. Carefully, I used a letter opener to tear the sturdy packaging. Inside was a letter from my fraternity. It was beautifully framed in a green velvet trim, matching the fraternity letterhead.

Dear Spence:

Thanks again for the <u>fantastic</u> presentation you gave before our Dallas Leadership Conference and for the incredible hospitality you showed to me, my staff, and our conference delegates.

You'll be happy to know that the delegates indicated on their evaluation forms that they felt that the Leadership Conference was an overwhelming success. You should also take pride in knowing that your speech that Friday evening was listed by many as the highlight of the weekend. I'm confident that everyone present recognized the vital role you played throughout the entire weekend in building the success of the program.

Spence, you have a fantastic story to tell. It's one that comes directly from the heart, which gives it all the more impact. I'll not soon forget the time we spent together, the meaningful discussions between us, and your grand hospitality. If ever I can repay the favor, please don't hesitate a second to call me personally.

With sincere best wishes in the fraternity.

Fraternally,
Dick
Richard A. Huebner
Executive Director

The instinctive pride evaporated when Don entered the office already speaking: "Spence, Fred Dean is on the line and said it was urgent; it is." As I turned to my right to take the phone, I let my eyes glance to the letter just once more. I paused and said to Lisa, "Could you please get me a picture hook so I can put up this frame?"

Lisa responded, "Sure."

I picked up the phone.

"Hello, Fred. What's up?"

A view from Fred Dean

"Hello, Fred. What's up?"

"Spence," I said, "you need to come up right away. I've got a real good friend on the team in real trouble, and I told him you could help him. He and several of the other guys went to a party, and one of the girls they had up there is saying that he and another teammate … you know…. Man, she's sayin' they raped her, Spence. It's bullshit, for sure. Anyway, the other guy's got an agent that's an attorney, but I met him once and he's a young hothead. He played football with our other teammate in college, but he wasn't that good at football, and I doubt he's any good as a lawyer. Our guy is afraid he'll make things worse, like, ya know, like, he'll fuck up. I'll pay your way, okay? Right now the team doesn't know squat. So please come."

"Fred," he said, "I'll get Lisa to set a flight for me. In the meantime, listen carefully. Tell your buddy not to talk about the case to anyone. No one, Fred. Not you, his mother, his priest, not God or Jesus … not a fucking soul. Have him get a hotel room and stay there until I arrive. Now, answer me this: are there any witnesses that can help him about what this girl is saying or about the girl's previous history with any other players? I want to guesstimate, based on what you tell me, if the accusation of this girl has a higher percentage of being legit or not."

I breathed heavily into the phone and then said, "From what I know, several guys know her, but I know there is one guy for sure."

"Okay, don't let your guy talk to that guy to try to influence him. We don't want the police to get the impression we are conducting ourselves inappropriately. You see, we want to be intelligently helpful to the police. At the same time, we don't want to jeopardize your buddy and expose him. When I get there, I'll deal with that young attorney. If he's like you say, you are probably right: he could fuck up this deal. One wrong step on his part could sure do that, I'm telling you straight. Fred, there is nothing more dangerous than someone who thinks they know enough about a subject and they know just enough to royally screw it up."

I hung up the phone and waited.

I picked up Spence at the National Airport and took him to a hotel in Reston, Virginia. That evening, we met with my friend, the accused, and he told Spence all the facts that he believed he was aware of. Spence once told me that people involved in similar situations have a tendency to subconsciously leave out pertinent facts. It's either because they are embarrassed to divulge them or they are so traumatized by the situation that they go temporarily numb and blank on some of the details. In any case, I knew we needed to keep the investigators from exposing my friend to the press. Once a man is accused of rape, he might as well have done it—it is a life-changing accusation, even for an innocent man.

I was more worried about the attorney that Spence was going to have to deal with. This guy was sensitive to Spence's mere arrival. He was a walking cliché: a lawyer who was more concerned about how cocksure he appeared in front of his high-profile client than he was about what was in his client's best interest. His conduct may not have been deliberate or thought out, but it was what it was. His conduct dripped with the thick syrup of conceit. And we soon found out how extremely hazardous he might have been to the overall plan of defense for both accused men.

We met at the hotel. There were two other professional football players in the room, and the attorney was bigger than both of them. Spence asked me to wait outside, and so I didn't know until later that the guy revealed to Spence that his plan was to go to the police station and assert the innocence of his client. I'm no lawyer, but even I know that would have been a mistake. Spence told me that he simply said the words "That would be a mistake," and the bigger lawyer began to throw a tantrum that would put John McEnroe to shame.

From outside, I heard the man say, "You motherfucker. Who do you think you are talking to? I should kick your fucking ass right now, you arrogant little shit!"

I threw open the door and charged inside, glared at him and said, "What the fuck are you doing? Are you a lawyer, man? Because this is my lawyer, and I've never seen bullshit like that come out of him. You'd do a lot better—and, believe me, you'll stay safer—not talking like that. In some other company, you could get hurt.... Besides, it makes you look like a little kid. It certainly makes you look like a low-class nothin'."

I turned and looked at Spence and then back at the other attorney and continued, "Look, man, I brought my guy all the way from Dallas because I know what he can do. I care what happens to my friends. Do you care what happens to yours?"

Spence had already started to gather his papers. The other man's client, almost in a whisper, asked my buddy where Spence was going, and Spence said, "I am leaving. If we can't be unified, there is no point in my being here. I'll tell you something point-blank: I offered to talk to your attorney alone, knowing this might happen, but he refused. He insisted that we meet with both of you present. Look, this isn't the playground or the football field. So I'm telling, not bragging, when I tell you that I have handled serious cases, including those of professional athletes, the charges of which ranged from child molestation and rape to murder. But I had help from more experienced attorneys back then, and I welcomed their assistance. Instead of hearing what I have to recommend and inviting my experience, you greet me and my client with a plan that scares me, frankly.

"First, you don't go down to the police department, unless your client has been arrested or it's public knowledge that your client has been charged. Right now, the press has no clue. They don't even know who is under investigation. Why don't you just take out an ad or rent a neon sign while you're at it? Why invite that on our clients? That is a real intelligent move, don't you think? Do you think if you go down to the police station to state your client is innocent, they are going to be more inclined to believe you? If it hits the papers, it will push the police in a direction—I assure you—that we don't want them to go down. Right now, they appear to be trying to seek the truth—whatever that means to the press—and they will dig deep into this accusation if the word gets out. And then they will … speculate. We need to help keep them off that path."

Spence finally breathed.

The other man stared with a reddened face—he knew he was wrong.

Before anyone could think, Spence continued, "We need a private meeting, away from the police station, with the Commonwealth Attorney. We need to conduct our own private polygraph tests and submit the results if they are positive. Otherwise, don't tell them shit. Obviously, some people, despite being innocent, get nervous about the test and come up with results that are inconclusive. We need to get a tester who is respected by the Commonwealth Police Department. And maybe even take a police polygraph with their knowing we passed a previous test by a polygrapher they respect. Until then, no police station. No press. Nothing. But you know that.…

"No," Spence said with a tinge of arrogance. "You do what you're thinking of doing, you will simply invite an indictment. There is a way we can avoid all of that … and I know what it is … and that's why I'm here."

A heavy chill filled the room. Spence turned and left the silence behind as he closed the door.

That evening, Fred received a call from the other teammate under suspicion. He indicated that I could take the lead in dealing with the police investigators and the Commonwealth Attorney. I would keep his representative informed, and we worked together amicably from that point forward.

I returned to Dallas briefly and then traveled back to Washington, where I remained for approximately ten days until the matter was successfully resolved on October 23, 1980. On October 24, the local media outlets and national sports stations reported what was written in the *Washington Star*:

> *"Fairfax Clears 2 Redskins In Rape Probe"*
> *by Christopher P. Winner*
> *Washington Star Staff Writer*
>
> *Fairfax County Commonwealth's Attorney Robert F. Horan, Jr. yesterday cleared two Redskins players who had been under investigation for more than two months in connection with the rape of a 20-year-old Reston woman.*
>
> *In a prepared statement, Horan said county police and prosecutors had conducted "intensive interviews" during the investigation. "No criminal charges are warranted in this case," the statement concluded.*
>
> *Neither Redskins Coach Jack Pardee nor Redskins team officials would comment on the outcome of the investigation.*
>
> *The prosecutor would not name the two players—believed to be starters—but said both had cooperated with police. "Intensive interviews were conducted with players, and one voluntarily underwent a polygraph test of nearly three hours," Horan said.*

It was not clear if the player who took the lie detector test was one of those under investigation, however.

Horan said he had discussed the case "in detail" with Fairfax Chief of Detectives James Joseph and Sex Crimes Section Chief Daniel Golhardt. "It is their conclusion that no criminal charges are warranted in this case," Horan said.

Neither prosecutors nor police officials would divulge the name of the Reston woman. Several Redskins players live in Reston because of its proximity to Redskins Park, where the team practices.

"I have no doubt whatsoever that there is insufficient evidence on which to base criminal accusations," Horan added.

Fairfax police spokesman Warren Carmichael yesterday refused to discuss the case and referred all inquiries to Horan's office. "This office will have nothing further to say on the matter," Carmichael said.

According to police sources, the incident under investigation occurred at a party on the night of Sept. 7—a day before the team's season-opener against the Dallas Cowboys—and involved at least two starting players.

When the existence of an investigation was revealed, one county prosecutor called the case "a high-profile situation with far-reaching ramifications for a lot of people."

CHAPTER 6
Attorney, Protector, Friend

A view from Norm Wells

It was approximately 2:00 a.m. on October 11, 1981. A group of us were at Café Dallas on Greenville Avenue in the Old Town Shopping Center. The Café had decent food and tall drinks, but (more importantly) seemed to attract beautiful women; we all loved to hang out there. As we were leaving, my roommate Don Smerek (a backup defensive lineman for the Dallas Cowboys) was having words with a guy who had apparently cut Don off with his car. Don was getting pretty pissed and started to bang on the hood of the guy's car, trying to coax him into coming out for a beating. Don kicked the driver's-side door, and the man behind the wheel rolled down his window and calmly pointed a pistol. Without saying a word, he fired one shot into Don's chest. We found out later that the bullet had entered Don's right lung and exited his body. Don would express to me later that it was like air being released from a balloon.

But at the time, it didn't seem to faze him. Don became angrier and attempted to chase down the car, which had driven off. I grabbed him and told him that we needed to get him to a hospital. I realized he was hurt badly and that time was of the essence if the doctors were to save his life. The ambulance arrived, and the paramedics immediately removed Don's shirt and placed it on the ground before attempting to move him. They examined his wound and began to work feverishly. Within minutes, they put Don in the ambulance and placed his shirt in a corner of the rear compartment.

As the ambulance drove away, people gathered around the scene of the shooting. A rumor circulated that a vial of drugs was seen on the ground right after the shooter had lowered his window. However, when the ambulance pulled away, there was no vial in sight.

After I reached the hospital, I immediately called Spence. Here is how I recall the conversation and the events subsequent to the shooting:

It was approximately 2:45 a.m. as the phone began to ring. On the fourth ring, Spence's fiancée, Cathy, answered in a very tired voice, "Hello."

I said, "Hello, Cathy. This is Norm, Norm Wells. Something terrible has happened. This is no joke, I promise. Please let me talk to Spence."

"Sweetie. It's Norm Wells. He said something terrible has happened," she said.

Although he sounded half-asleep, Spence jumped me pretty good for calling so late. "Hey, Norm. What's the gag? It's nearly three o'clock. Don't mess with Cathy that way."

"Spence, this ain't no gag. Donnie's been shot. We were at Café Dallas, and he just got shot in the parking lot. I am at the hospital right now. You need to get down here right away. There's talk that there were drugs found. But I was holding him in my arms, and

I would have felt it because I was unbuttoning his shirt when the ambulance arrived—he was clean. I grabbed his wallet, his cash, and his car keys."

"Look, keep your cool. How bad was he hit?" Spence asked.

"He was shot in the left chest. Based on what Donnie said to me, it was probably his right lung."

"Wait a minute. You just said he was shot in the left chest. How could that be his right lung?"

"I'm sorry," I said. "I'm disoriented, man. I was describing how I was looking at him. He—he was hit on the right side of his chest. It was the right lung. Spence—the police are here questioning everyone. What should I do?"

"All right, listen to me very carefully—focus on what I am saying," he said intensely. "Take a few breaths, Norm.... If someone comes up to you, ignore 'em till we're finished. But if you have to talk, first thing to remember: talk very slowly. Pause quite a bit, like your mind is wandering. You can do this, Norm. You went to Northwestern for God's sake; you're a smart guy. You can do this. Remember, I am coming from Allen, so it will take me thirty minutes, worst case. Buy me some time by telling them you need to calm down. If they push you to issue a statement, just remember to talk slowly and generally, kinda like you're making an excuse for Laurie when you come home late. If they then start to press you, tell them directly, and even firmly, for them not to. Reiterate that your roommate—your best friend—just got shot. Just tell them that they need to back off a bit. Try to be polite, but don't let them press you. Be apologetic and tell them that you understand that they are just doing their job, but that they need to understand the circumstances and what everyone close to Don is going through. If you play it right, and I know you can, I should get there in time to take over. Understand this: they want to catch that bastard just as much as you do. So make them address your concerns about the shooter and not Don for now."

"What about the other stuff. You know?"

"I'll deal with that when I get there. Don't you even try to deal with that. Get me the numbers for Donnie's parents. I'll handle those calls with you. There are certain things I need to do for Don that will require their cooperation. And I will need that cooperation fast. Understand?"

"I understand. Just hurry."

"I am walking out the door."

Spence arrived at the hospital in about eighteen minutes. I couldn't believe it. He had to be flying low to get there that fast. As he walked through the doors of the emergency room, a sense of calm overcame all of us who were waiting. He greeted everyone and then quickly excused himself to deal with the police. While we were happy Spencer had arrived, all of Don's teammates and friends felt helpless. It was a horrendous feeling. We were worried for Donnie, and we were worried about what was going on with the police. The police seemed to be more concerned about Donnie's conduct at the scene of the shooting than they were with the fact that he had been shot. That pissed us off. Nothing Donnie did justified his getting shot.

After about an hour or so, Spence returned to the waiting room. He wouldn't share with us what transpired in his conversations with the police (although later we found out that he had done a masterful job in protecting Donnie). Spence handled the press as well. He got those guys to just describe the situation without trying to overspeculate, as the press can always be counted on to do. And the police refused to issue a speculative opinion on what happened. I wonder who got them to refrain from doing that.

Then, as we all sat there, Spence said something that drew a smile to almost all of our faces and even a few giggles: "Look, everyone," he said, "I already sent a message to my buddy upstairs, and he said Donnie will be just fine. Oh, you all didn't know that I have a direct pipeline to him, too? Well, y'all should know better."

Spence and I excused ourselves, and we contacted Donnie's parents. Spence needed a Specific Power of Attorney to stand in Donnie's place and protect his best interests. He was given that authority over the telephone before witnesses and received the signed documentation the next day.

Spence and I went up to Donnie's room. Spence was the only one permitted inside—absolutely no one else except hospital staff. That meant everyone—so I waited outside the room.

As the night turned into early morning, Gil Brandt, the team's Player Personnel Director, came to Donnie's room. He attempted to push open the door, and the nurse inside interceded, pointing to the sign next to the jamb: *Absolutely No Visitors*. She told him that other than the hospital staff, there were no visitors permitted without Mr. Kopf's permission. Gil asserted that he was from the Dallas Cowboys, the man in charge of player personnel, and that he was there in Don's best interest as Don's employer. The nurse slipped back into the room, and Spence came out a moment later. He greeted Gil respectfully and then said, "Gil, as Don's attorney and family representative, I am limiting visitations to family and clergy."

"Look, I've come here as the representative of the Dallas Cowboys, and I want to see my player," Gil said firmly.

With that, Spence looked Gil sternly in the eyes and said, "Gil, I appreciate that, believe me I do. However, I care more about my client and friend's well-being—his health and legal well-being. If he were to exclaim an *excited utterance* with you in the room, you would be a potential witness in a court proceeding. I don't want to have to deal with that, and neither would Tex. I will give your best wishes to Don, and I will keep your office informed of his progress. That's the best I can do."

"Look, there's no good reason for me not to see Don," Gil replied.

"Listen," said Spence in a low voice, just above a whisper. "I don't want this to become adversarial. However, you're the only one who is attacking. I know the true reason why you are pressing me has nothing to do with Don. And that is unfortunate. I'm sorry that you can't see that I am not treating you any differently from anyone else. Even his roommate can't visit him. Quite frankly, Don's doctors have it so that the only visitor allowed is me until his parents arrive from Nevada. Now, please tell Tex I'll call him if there is any significant change." With that, Spence turned to re-enter Don's hospital room.

Gil responded, "This is bull."

Without hesitation, Spence turned and replied, "I'm an attorney doing a difficult job, and you're not making the job any easier. You know, Gil, you need to shelve your insecurities and your being so damn sensitive. This crap that is happening now in this hospital, in that room, is not about you or what your job responsibilities are or who you work for. It's about a young man fighting for his life. His life, Gil. If you really cared about him, you wouldn't be busting my ass. So, meaning no disrespect, I'll call you later when Don is coherent and capable of receiving visitors. Thanks again for coming." He went back into Donnie's room and quietly closed the door.

Gil never forgave Spence for that rebuff. In fact, he despised him for it and could never let it go. He had to know Spence had no choice, but that didn't matter to Gil. He also blatantly acted as if he resented that both Coach Landry and Tex liked and respected Spence for all that he had done for the players and the Cowboys as a whole. Even Gil's own secretary, Tula, came to know and love Spence. Gil knew that Spence did all of our contracts with Tex or Coach, depending upon the situation. That infuriated him. It had nothing to do with Spence as a person. It was just that Spence knew Gil's true position in the organization, and Spence didn't like to have his time wasted.

I was present several times when Coach called Spence directly at home to discuss a player. To my knowledge, at that time, except for Randy White's agent Howard Slusher, who dealt with Tex for one specific contract negotiation, Spencer was the only rep afforded that courtesy and respect on a continuous basis. I wish everyone we knew could have seen it. It was impressive watching him shield Donnie like a lion protecting its cub. I respected what Spence was doing and never questioned his expertise or the reasons why he conducted himself the way he did, ever. He demanded respect and got it.

A few hours later, Coach Landry came to Donnie's hospital room. Spence was informed by one of the nurses that Coach Landry was outside. He came out and warmly greeted Coach. There was a mutual respect between them, but it clearly was more than just respect and business. They liked each other. Anyway, Coach Landry then greeted me and started a short conversation with Spence that went something like this:

"Spence, how is he doing? Still no visitors?" Coach asked in that slight South Texas drawl.

"Well, he's been out for quite some time. But because of the investigation, it limits my ability to permit visitors. Presently, he is stable and sleeping soundly."

"All of us with the team are obviously very concerned, especially Ernie Stautner," said Coach.

"I appreciate that, and I know Don would. You both mean a great deal to him. You know that he respects you both very much."

"I was hoping I could visit with Don and pray with him if it's all right with you."

"Coach, if you want to pray with Don, that's fine. I'm sure he would be proud if you did. Please understand that I need to be present in the event Don makes any *excited utterances*. If that should start to occur, I would be compelled to have to ask you to leave the room abruptly. For your sake and for Don's sake as well. I tried to explain that to Gil, but he wouldn't buy it."

"Well, Spence, I appreciate this very much," Coach said. "Gil will understand. He's just trying to do his job, and he is not used to dealing with someone with your sense of directness. He is used to getting his way. That's why he gets a bit frustrated with you. I'm sure you understand."

"I understand, Coach," Spence said.

"Believe me when I say that I completely understand what you are trying to do for Don and all the fellas you help. You're looking out for their best interests, and you do a great job. Obviously, our people have firsthand knowledge of that."

With that, Coach entered the room and sat down next to Don. I peeked through the doorway. Donnie's seemingly invincible body lay motionless with tubes in his veins, one down his throat, and monitors all around him. Spence was over in the corner, sitting silently. And then I saw Coach Landry's eyes fill with tears as he sat there holding Don's hand. He began to pray. Don slept. I was overwhelmed.

After he finished his prayer, Coach Landry sat quietly holding Don's hand for nearly fifteen minutes. He then rose to his feet, thanked Spence for permitting him to visit Don, and asked that Spence call him if there was any change or any problems with the Cowboys' staff, including Gil. We all found out that Coach didn't like or respect agents or representatives—that is, except for our man. If you don't believe it, you can ask Coach Ditka, Coach Mackovic, or Coach Stallings. They'll all tell you the same.

Spence never left Don's side, not even to eat, until Donnie's parents entered his room. He had private words with Donnie that brought me to tears when Don later shared them with me. Donnie loved Spence. Not because of how he handled this crisis. Not because he did his legal work. Not because he busted the bank of the Dallas Cowboys, making Donnie the highest-paid backup defensive lineman in Dallas Cowboys' history. He loved him because he was always there. Regardless of the issue or the odds, Spence would be there.

The next day, it circulated around the locker room what had happened to Don and how well Donnie's man had handled the entire situation (the police, the press, and the Cowboys). All the guys that Spence had helped strutted around the barracks like peacocks bragging about their guy and comparing him to our other teammates' reps. As I was getting ready for practice, Coach Landry came by my locker and asked how I was doing. Then he put his arm on my shoulder and said, "Norm, you should be proud of the way you handled yourself yesterday. Don should be proud of you, too." Then, as he started to walk toward the door leading to the practice field, he stopped, turned back to me for a second, and with a rare warm smile, said, "Oh, and your guy Spence: he's *top shelf.*"

At the time, to be honest, I didn't know what Coach meant by *top shelf*; but now that I know, he couldn't have been more right. Coach Landry had a knack of saying a great deal with very few words. As for me, I leave the description of what Spence did for Don that night up to the expertise and style of the great college basketball commentator Dick Vitale, who simply would have said, "He was *awesome*, baby! With a capital A."

Joe: You know what the problem is? It's that the media doesn't tell it like it is, if they tell it at all. So we go on the radio, on Real Sports, and they ask the right questions, and the word gets out.... But these leaders and their handpicked cronies should have been *fired*! It's just not open to speculation anymore. Tell me: who keeps a $28 million team of deliberate screwups? Now, remember Dave Smith— remember what Spence said about him the other night, B. J.?

Billy Joe: Yeah. If he hadn't been ballsy enough to print that thing, Spence and I never would have teamed up. This probably never would have broken from the barroom chatter. Remember him from the *Dallas Morning News*, Tony? Dave Smith?

Tony: Sure: sports editor extraordinaire.

Joe: He had some stones to print that copy, man. Stones....

CHAPTER 7
The Dave Smith

A view from Spencer Kopf

After court, I ran over to see Judge Richard Mays to say hi and use his phone in the quiet. Mays was a highly respected jurist, and it was he who had sat in judgment in The State of Texas v. Michael Hegman. I poked my head into the judge's chambers, and he said, "Need to use the phone, Spence?"

I replied, "You guessed it.... All the pay phones are locked up in the hall again."

"No problem," he said. "I have to sneak out for a minute. If I'm not back by the time you're finished, just shut the door on your way out."

"Thanks, Judge," I said, as he removed his robes, hung them on the hat rack, and strolled out quickly.

I called Lisa for my messages and an update on my appointments scheduled for that day. She was as direct and thorough as always:

"Your lunch appointment with Pete Vouras is pushed to tomorrow, if it's okay with you. Your two o'clock with that new corporate client is pushed to three, and Cathy needs you to meet her at the caterer's at half-past-five. And last, Dave Smith called and asked that you call him to see if you could meet him before lunch or join him for lunch if you can. He said to tell you it was important and that lunch would be on him."

"What's Dave's number? I left my planner on my desk."

"What else is new? Check to see if you left your wallet in your desk like you did yesterday, in case I have to bring it to you," she said, laughing.

"Wise guy. I've got my wallet and my pen and my business cards, and my head is still on. Please call Cathy and tell her I will be on time. Now, what's Dave's number, please?"

I called Dave Smith, then sports editor of the *Dallas Morning News*; formerly, he had held the same position with the *Boston Globe* and *Washington Star*. A special edition of *Sports Illustrated* listed the fifty most influential moments in sports in the last fifty years: the appointment of Dave Smith as sports editor of a major newspaper was listed as number eighteen. Smith was as sharp as they come. He had impeccable integrity, he was brilliant, and he would take every dime you had if you dared to play him in tennis. And he was a strong confidant, a good friend.

Dave picked up the phone himself. "Hello. Dave Smith."

I responded, "Rod Laver, please."

"What do you say, big guy?"

"All right. Cut to it, Dave. You called me. What do you want?" I asked. "You didn't call me Short Guy, so you must want something."

"Look, I need your undivided attention. No phones. We need to go somewhere."

"There had better be sandwiches where we're going."

He chuckled. "I'm buying."

Before I left, I said my good-byes to Judge Mays. He was talking to his court coordinator, so I stuck my head in during a slightly extended pause in their conversation to thank him for the phone. He just said, "Keep pluggin'."

On the elevator, Judge Ron Chapman and I chatted. He was my closest buddy at the courthouse and a well-respected judge. In fact, two months later when I received my appointment to the bench, he surprised me with judge's robes, the most overwhelming and thoughtful gift I have ever received. We shook hands, and I walked briskly to my car. The entire ride, I thought about what Dave could possibly want.

As I checked through security at the *Dallas Morning News* building, I was given a visitor's badge to clip to my lapel. The security guard told me the floor, and I took the elevator up to the sports department. A young lady escorted me to Dave's office, winding through the thunderous clap of typewriter keyboards and chatting sportswriters. Dave's office was a glass panopticon—he could see the entire floor. Papers appeared to be strewn over the furniture of his modestly decorated office, but there was somehow order to it all. He looked up as I entered, half grinning. No hello.

"Tell me," he uttered, "what does someone have to do to straighten out the poor excuse for leadership of the union ... what does someone have to do to make some greedy, heartless owners do the right thing? What do you think about this strike that's coming?"

I said, "Dave, hello to you, too. But if you've gotta know, I think that the strike shouldn't occur now, certainly not this season. Not because it shouldn't in principle or isn't necessary—it's that the players and the union aren't ready. Not financially. Not emotionally.

Furthermore, this union leadership has an arrogance that has created an aura of distrust among a large portion of the union's membership. These leaders are seeking unachievable financial goals instead of the necessities like health benefits, disability benefits, and matching pension funds by the owners. They should be seeking achievable goals like these. Realistically achievable salary upgrades commensurate with the other sports should be their aim, but these union leaders are asking for the world. And they are pressing the union members that they allow the union to represent them with their individual employment contracts with the teams, instead of having their own personal representatives. It's just plain idiocy. This should be the opportune time to get basic benefits that the players should have, but don't."

Dave adamantly interrupted, "You're writing a column about this for this Sunday's sports commentary page."

"I don't write columns," I said.

He glared at me and tonelessly, like a high school chemistry teacher, he said, "I expect a thousand words about this strike on my desk by Thursday at five to make Sunday's paper." He moved a stack of pages over to reveal two sandwiches and bags of chips. "Hungry?"

"Did you know sometimes you're a real putz?"

"I believe I've been told that on more than one occasion. Come on, think of all the fun you'll have venting those feelings we've been talking about these past months."

"Okay, but just the one article."

"Absolutely, just this once," he said insincerely.

I headed back to the office to draft Don to collaborate.

CHAPTER 8
The Article

SPENCER W. KOPF
<u>Guest Columnist</u>

Ed Garvey, the high-visibility executive director of the National Football League Players Association, has drawn considerable media attention by his statements concerning the imminent demise of the NFLPA's Collective Bargaining Agreement.

The gospel according to Garvey is as follows: July 15 marks the end of the Collective Bargaining Agreement and the end of the player's personal right to choose his own representative to negotiate his contract. From Garvey's perspective, this will mark a new era of "protection" for the players. Garvey speaks of setting standards and the protection of the players in the same breath, as though the two were somehow linked.

Viewed from a more realistic perspective, Mr. Garvey's assertion will not bear close scrutiny. It is the function of the NFLPA to establish minimum base salaries for all players, the protection of the existing pension plan, protection of the players' medical benefits and, hopefully in the future, the establishment of medical standards to protect the players from unscrupulous teams and their staff doctors and establishment of true free agency. Those are the protective standards to which the NFLPA should be striving.

The elimination of individual representatives from the players is not a protective measure for those players but rather a harmful development, which will retard football players from achieving parity with other professional athletes.

Football players fall far behind their brethren in basketball and baseball when it comes to sharing the sports dollars. It is a tribute to the NFL management and an indictment of the NFLPA that the existing base salary is so low that players' representatives have a poor foundation to build their negotiations upon.

The NFLPA should work to raise the base to a realistic level so that all players could improve their positions. No major sport has a percentage-of-the-gross provision, yet their average salaries far exceed those in football.

Much like actors, athletes are unique individuals with unique talents and values. Like actors, athletes should be protected by minimum scale compensation, but should also be able to individually bargain for their talents.

Unions are geared to protect their weakest member. Just as the minimum scale of Actor's Equity could in no way justly compensate a Marlon Brando, neither could the minimum standards of the NFLPA adequately compensate a superstar of the O.J. Simpson caliber. Unique individuals require the unique attention of their own personal representatives. While the NFLPA can serve a useful function in establishing minimum standards, it cannot adequately serve the interest of its more talented members.

The NFLPA is addressing the renegotiating of its Collective Bargaining Agreement with PATCO-like demands. If pursued with the same finesse, a PATCO-like result may await members of the NFLPA. The players need the protection of a Collective Bargaining Agreement; they do not need an overzealous negotiating position that paints them into a corner from which there is no escape. The teams are eagerly urging players to defect from the NFLPA. Membership has never been unanimous, and the prospect of union-negotiated salaries will further deplete the ranks.

Who is Ed Garvey who yearns to speak for 1,170 professional football players? He is the man most responsible for the terms of the 1977 Collective Bargaining Agreement, the agreement which failed to adequately consider inflation, resulting in a pseudo free-agency which required a team seeking to sign a free agent to compensate his old team with a first-found draft choice if the free agent made or was offered as much as $80,000 in 1981. The average reported salary in the NFL exceeds $80,000, making it practically impossible for all but the superstars to achieve free-agent status and take their talent where it is appreciated most.

The current Collective Bargaining Agreement has its obvious shortcomings and clearly needs to be vigorously renegotiated. The question arises: how effectively can Mr. Garvey bargain for 1,170 individual players while he is fighting for a new and more effective Collective Bargaining Agreement?

Mr. Garvey proposes to "protect" the players by embarking upon a monumental division of labor, negotiating a contract for the union and contracts for all the players simultaneously. This form of treatment would reduce individual consideration for the players to the cattle-call mentality of another era. That cattle-call outlook is evidenced by the fact that there is one base salary for all players, regardless of position. Athletes are not cattle, they are individuals. Individuals deserve individual treatment. Mr. Garvey derides all player representatives without regard for their character and ability, and also removing the incentive to perform to the players' maximum potential. Garvey's proposal would level salaries and stifle the urge to excel. The new Collective Bargaining Agreement should preserve players' rights to individual representation. The union is supposed to protect the players from management; who will protect the players from the union?

(Spencer Kopf is a Dallas-based attorney who is well versed in sports law and who has been handling professional athletes, eight of whom are Dallas Cowboys, since 1976.)

Garvey garbling player issues

SPENCER W. KOPF
Guest Columnist

Ed Garvey, the high visibility executive director of the National Football League Players Association, has drawn considerable media attention by his statements concerning the imminent demise of the NFLPA's Collective Bargaining Agreement.

The gospel according to Garvey is as follows: July 15th marks the end of the Collective Bargaining Agreement and the end of the player's personal right to choose his own representative to negotiate his contract. From Garvey's perspective, this will mark a new era of "protection" for the players. Garvey speaks of setting standards and the protection of the players in the same breath as though the two were somehow linked.

Viewed from a more realistic perspective, Mr. Garvey's assertion will not bear close scrutiny. It is the function of the NFLPA to establish minimum base salaries for all players, the protection of the existing pension plan, protection of the players medical benefits and, hopefully in the future, the establishment of medical standards to protect the players from unscrupulous teams and their staff doctors and establishment of true free agency. Those are the protective standards to which the NFLPA should be striving.

The elimination of individual representatives for the players is not a protective measure for those players but rather a harmful development which will retard football players from achieving parity with other professional athletes.

Football players fall far behind their brethren in basketball and baseball when it comes to sharing the sports dollars. It is a tribute to the NFL management and an indictment of the NFLPA that the existing base salary is so low that players' representatives have a poor foundation to build their negotiations upon.

The NFLPA should work to raise the base to a realistic level so that all players could improve their positions. No major sport has a percentage-of-the-gross provision, yet their average salaries far exceed those in football.

Much like actors, athletes are unique individuals with unique talents and values. Like actors, athletes should be protected by minimum scale compensation, but should also be able to individually bargain for their talents.

Unions are geared to protect their weakest member. Just as the minimum scale of Actor's Equity could in no way justly compensate a Marlon Brando, neither could the minimum standards of the NFLPA adequately compensate a superstar of the O.J. Simpson caliber. Unique individuals require the unique attention of their own personal representatives. While the NFLPA can serve a useful function in establishing minimum standards, it cannot adequately serve the interest of its more talented members.

The NFLPA is addressing the re-negotiating of its Collective Bargaining Agreement with PATCO-like demands. If pursued with the same finesse, a PATCO-like result may await members of the NFLPA. The players need the protection of a Collective Bargaining Agreement, they do not need an overzealous negotiating position that paints them into a corner from which there is no escape. The teams are eagerly urging players to defect from the NFLPA. Membership has never been unanimous, and the prospect of union negotiated salaries will further deplete the ranks.

Who is Ed Garvey who yearns to speak for 1,170 professional football players? He is the man most responsible for the terms of the 1977 Collective Bargaining Agreement, the agreement which failed to adequately consider inflation, resulting in a pseudo free-agency which requires a team seeking to sign a free agent to compensate his old team with a first-round draft choice if the free agent made or was offered as much as $80,000 in 1981. The average reported salary in the NFL exceeds $80,000, making it practically impossible for all but the superstars to achieve free-agent status and take their talent where it is appreciated most.

The current Collective Bargaining Agreement has its obvious shortcomings and clearly needs to be vigorously renegotiated. The question arises: How effectively can Mr. Garvey bargain for 1,170 individual players while he is fighting for a new and more effective Collective Bargaining Agreement?

Mr. Garvey proposes to "protect" the players by embarking upon a monumental division of labor, negotiating a contract for the union and contracts for all the players simultaneously. This form of treatment would reduce individual consideration for the players to the cattle-call mentality of another era. That cattle-call outlook is evidenced by the fact that there is one base salary for all players, regardless of position. Athletes are not cattle, they are individuals. Individuals deserve individual treatment. Mr. Garvey derides all player representatives without regard for their character and ability and also removing the incentive to perform to the players maximum potential. Garvey's proposal would level salaries and stifle the urge to excel. The new Collective Bargaining Agreement should preserve players' rights to individual representation. The union is supposed to protect the players from management, who will protect the players from the union?

(Spencer Kopf is a Dallas-based attorney who is well-versed in sports law and who has been handling professional athletes, eight of whom are Dallas Cowboys, since 1976.)

Tony: You know, if this strike does break out soon, the one thing that will be different is how set up even the third stringers are this time around. I mean, I don't know what you guys were paid, but it wasn't much. And the worst part back then was the *trust* that all these players had in the union leaders. These guys were telling them: "No need for personal lawyers. No need to see those confusing documents. No need to watch the watchers. We'll take care of you." And why not believe them if all you can focus on is dying to play in the pros?

Billy Joe: Have you met Anthony Dickerson?

Tony: Uh.… Not sure.

Billy Joe: He's a great guy; what you just said is his story, man. Same thing. Remember how racked with nerves the camps were? The Cowboys' camp was nuts. I mean, I knew that I could be okay, for a while at least; by then, I had my own construction business. But some of those guys were not only scared shitless of never getting their job back, but this thing was strung out so long that most of these guys were literally suffering.

Joe: Yeah, and now all those guys who were dragged through the grime of that strike by the leaders they trusted are retired now and just swept under the rug. Nothing's changed.

Billy Joe: Could you imagine if Brett Favre's having a car were actually contingent on whether or not a strike got dragged out longer? Say that happened and the NFLPA did nothing about it. While Favre, meanwhile, has to—where was Anthony working? Oh, yeah, a hotel watering plants to make ends meet. Imagine Brett watering plants during a strike 'cause his cash's run out, winning the Super Bowl a few years later, and then twenty years down the line denied adequate pension and health benefits. Imagine that....

CHAPTER 9
Training Camp

Commentary by Spencer Kopf

High levels of stress and anger were consuming every team's roster throughout the National Football League when the training camps opened. The media and press had given nicknames to a number of camps based on the turbulent aura surrounding the practice fields. The Dallas Cowboys were "Team Discontent," and statements from several of the team's employees justified that label. Half a dozen veterans of that roster had shown open, vocal disgust with the upper management, stressing the inadequacy of player salaries and bonuses.

The Cowboys' office, and others, openly sparred with player comments by justifying their business position directly and sharply. One executive claimed, "[I]f you ask 100 players, 99 would say they are underpaid."[4] But continued to say, "All I know is the money being offered is fair and just."[5] Those remarks were far from the most

4   Myers, "Dutton's Disgusted."
5   Ibid.

thought-out or intelligent comments to be made by a team official. That stance not only revealed a conscious indifference for accuracy, juxtaposing those two ideas revealed the cynicism and acquisitiveness that we all expected the owners held secretly. In February of that year, the salaries of that team roster had appeared in a detailed article on the front page of the sports section of the *Dallas Morning News*. The article showed—plainly, unmistakably—how grossly underpaid the players were.

The aggressive tone that a few of the owners took in response did not endear them to public sentiment or to the members of the press and media. Meanwhile, the players were revealing to union representatives, friends, family, and others that coaching staffs were openly berating them and their teammates. The players were being accused of "dogging it" in practice and during preseason games as if they were already on strike. The strike hadn't started; and while none of the players I knew were disrespecting their game, every camp undoubtedly had an atmosphere of uncertainty and anxiety as to when the strike would commence.

Several of the players checked into the office every day to describe their daily routines. They reported that management was enticing the players to sign new contracts with (small) signing bonuses before the collective bargaining agreement expired on July 15. The management's attempt to buy them off cheaply and keep them under the poor, lower-salary structure of the old agreement was, to say the very least, a shameful, insulting ploy.

The more seasoned the veteran, the more exasperated he rightly was. John Dutton (a Dallas Cowboys' starting defensive lineman and former all-pro) and his teammate, the starting tight end Billy Joe DuPree, were *grossly* underpaid for their talent and performance. They were stuck in outdated, deplorably unconscionable contracts near the twilight of their highly successful careers, which made the uncaring and unappreciative treatment by the management even more disheartening. John and B. J. were faced with the unenviable position of having to threaten retirement or play out their contracts. Both knew that the management had younger players waiting in the wings who would naively accept anything to play professional football.

The union leadership had patently espoused ("in the best interest of the players") a desire to represent each player during his individual employment contract negotiations. Under this new proposal, player-selected agents and attorneys would no longer be permitted to participate, let alone advise their clients, during the contracting stage. The NFLPA executive director, Mr. Garvey, was an attorney with labor experience, and he undoubtedly knew, or should have known, the Code of Professional Responsibility. So, he was either incompetently unaware that a union's representing all three tight ends on the Cowboys was an obvious conflict of interest, in violation of the code of his honorable vocation; or he knew the code and chose to ignore it simply because it didn't apply to union representatives. The very first thing a lawyer does when a client walks into his office is a conflicts check—the greenest attorneys know this. Back then, however, agents had no code by which their conduct was judged. Perhaps Mr. Garvey assumed that he could circumvent the conflict issue by asserting that the union was not *really* acting as an attorney, but merely as an "agent." In any case, he placed every player in the NFLPA in greater jeopardy than had already existed even before he had proposed his so-called solution. Players did not have to have gone to law school to know this deal was shoddy, and many naturally felt and voiced that they would go to court to assert their rights to hire independent attorneys or representatives. And more players remained or became disgruntled as to why the union was unable to achieve proper medical coverage and disability benefits for its members.

Eventually, certain players requested that the union seek a one-year extension to the present collective bargaining agreement or go without one for a season, rather than strike. The players knew they did not have the financial capacity or leverage to sustain a strike for very long; some even wanted the membership to agree to sit out until the United States Football League became a viable option. Tempers rose and became short. On the practice fields, on a daily basis, adversarial discussions nearly became physical altercations. The message was clear from the owners that there would be no concessions and no movement unless they were somehow forced to do so. The owners must have felt untouchable. But both sides of the strike would come to understand that life—as Snoopy the beagle would say—is full of rude awakenings.

CHAPTER 10
Inside One Camp

A view from Anthony Dickerson

We landed at LAX for training camp, which was being held in Thousand Oaks, California. One hundred and twenty fellow rookies and I were competing for a handful of spots. Making the team would mean having to be the rookie in camp with the best combination of speed, tackling skill, and aggressive play. I just put it in my head that I was going to be the best rookie prospect in recent history. The team had lost Hollywood Henderson the previous year, so as far as I was concerned, the spot he left was mine. At least, that was the plan....

The veterans came about two weeks later. When they arrived, there were about ninety rookies left to battle the veterans for positions on the team. I was assigned to run and play with the seventh string; my plan had been hindered. The whistle was often blown just after the sixth-string players would perform, and the coaches never bothered with the seventh. On those days when I had no chance to show my best stuff, I made sure the coaches saw that I won every sprint or conditioning drill, on the chance that they would not cut a guy who was outhustling everyone else. And on the rare days when I was given a chance to perform, I was an animal: I hit during no-hit drills, dove for balls I had little chance of catching. The coaching staff took notice, once or twice scolding me for when I used game contact. But I wanted to give the impression that I would not back down.

I made it all the way to the first preseason game. My plan for that thrilling experience was to be outstanding on special teams' play. The Cowboys were big on handouts—they liked communication by memo. The handout sheets listed all the players on special teams. I looked the handout over, and my name was nowhere on the list. If your name was not on the list, you were free to go back to your room and go to bed. My fellow rookies, who were also not on the special team lists, were happy to go to their beds after a week of twice-a-day practices. They had no plan. I went to the meeting anyway.

Coach Mike Ditka was at the chalkboard. Scrawled on the slate were Xs and Os labeled with players' names. Ditka ordered quiet in Ditka fashion. The room went silent. I could hear the sound of gum chewing coming from across the room. He called out each player's name on the board. Each player signaled his presence by saying "yeah" or "here" or by simply grunting. He came to a player on the kickoff team. He did not respond to the roll call. Ditka repeated his name and still received no answer. I shouted, "Coach, I'll play it."

Ditka said, "Who said that?"

I stood up and said fervently, "Dickerson, Anthony."

He said, "Okay, Dickerson, you're the five-man on the kickoff team."

I repeated the same tack for every missing player I could—all those sleeping beauties. By the end of the meeting, I was on practically every special team for the upcoming game—mission accomplished.

I made the team and performed as one of the best pre-season special teams' players. I would start on pass defense, or four-O defense, as it was called, eventually making the All-Rookie Team, and was voted Dallas Cowboy Special Team Player of the Year. The next season, I was on the plane with the veterans.

I had just come from a great rookie season with America's team, the Dallas Cowboys. That off-season, after the Super Bowl, I treated myself to a vacation, spending a week in Honolulu watching some of my friends and teammates play in the Pro Bowl. It was a week of luxury hotels and rental cars, which were brand new commodities for me. A first-class reward, I thought, for making the team. By the time that vacation was over, however, there was rumor of a strike: no season and no paycheck. I had not planned for this. I had certainly known what I had to do to make the team, and what I was going to do with the money. But I had no strike plan.

That second trip I made to LAX for my second camp with the Cowboys was the most exciting flight I have ever taken. But when I touched down on the tarmac, it hit me that I was but a bus ride away from the hell of two-a-days. On the bus, I was soaking up the joking and the camaraderie when the tone quickly went from jovial to serious. Someone on the bus had mentioned the word *strike*. The conversations turned to foreclosures, repossessed cars, and even one-year "vacations" from the game. Last year I had a plan to play professional football. This year I had no plan to stay in the game. I feared that this situation was going to change or ruin families and lives. I hadn't saved my bread. I shouldn't have gone to watch the Super Bowl in New Orleans. I shouldn't have gone on vacation to Hawaii. I should have saved more. I should have planned....

The bus became quiet for half of the ride to Thousand Oaks. The upcoming strike ruined our camp from day one. Everyone practiced knowing that we might go weeks or months without pay. The last day of training was approaching, and each player knew he would have to maintain top physical shape on his own during the strike, all while compounding his attention with one worry after another. As a young man, I had been without money, so I figured the strike wouldn't be anything I wasn't used to; and since I had no family, home, car, or wife depending on me, I could handle bill collectors. But for most others, some days of practice were far from fun—with that kind of worry on players' minds, some of our practices were pitiful. Still, most of our practices were what one should expect of a championship team with two or three Hall of Famers, six to eight All-Pros, and eager youngsters like me who were hungry for our shot at the Super Bowl. And this is what depressed me the most: this was a great team with a great coach, and it looked like the impending strike was going to stop us from our destiny.

Our team meeting one evening started out with the typical routine. Coach Landry called roll and stated who would be fined for not following rules. There were, however, a few in the room who looked like football players, only they were strangely garbed in suits instead of sweats. They looked out of place and uncomfortable. Word came around that these were union reps: Upshaw and Company. The coaches left the room, and Upshaw and Company took the floor.

Upshaw began to talk about the owners' not sharing profits, their not providing insurance, and so forth. His comments brought anger and tension into the room. Many players were furious. Some started shouting. In the din of their overlapping questions, I was caught in a horrible daydream of no season, no paycheck, and no plan. Upshaw brought some relief when he asserted that the union would have funds for members for emergencies, and I immediately thought, *Where do I sign?* That sounded like my best plan for now. Upshaw left, and so it was back to business; there was a bit more from the coaches, and then we headed back to our rooms for rest and to discuss strike tactics. Younger players sat with older players asking for advice; phone calls went out to wives and loved ones. It was not a restful night.

The next practice left a bitter taste in the mouths of us players. By then, the consensus was that the owners were screwing us, and many were sure the coaches were on the owners' side. Not only would the strike mean no work and no money, some pointed out; it would be a paid vacation for the coaches and the rest of the staff. As prophetic as statements like this one seemed, we had little time to develop a reassuring strike plan; the rest of time at camp was filled with continual up-and-down practices and worried calls to home about where the money was going to come from to pay our bills. We weren't ready for a strike, and the owners knew it. We all managed to survive camp; however, the opening day revelation was that the strike could be as soon as two weeks away and that all of us could be out of work for a year.

The Monday before our first game, Coach Landry called roll. He then proudly appointed Danny White offensive team captain, Randy White defensive team captain, and me, Anthony Dickerson, special teams captain. That was one of the best days of my life. My teammates began to chant, "Dick, Dick, way to go, Dick." I considered that kind of respect from peers and coaches a reward for all of my hard work and rookie planning. Then, snap! Again the realization hit that this achievement would last for only two games; the rest of the season could be lost in the strike. *So much for my finest moment in sports*, I thought. I suddenly felt guilty for having a selfish thought, something that does not belong in a team sport. But the strike was starting to divide everyone on this team.

My analysis of the situation changed drastically with the help of some veterans. I decided to seek an alternative plan with that same assertiveness I had during my rookie season. In the process, I would become blessed to make cherished, lifelong friendships. And I would come to value, with a newfound deep appreciation, the awesomeness of a fellow alumnus of SMU, a man whose stature in my book has no equal.

Billy Joe DuPree: One guy that never let me down was our union rep, Robert Newhouse. Talk about a smart guy. Know what he's up to now? He's the trustee for the federal bankruptcy court here in Dallas. He's the epitome of integrity and trust. He was a good friend, just too often the bearer of bad news....

CHAPTER 11
Don't Shoot the Messenger

A view from Robert Newhouse

If anyone, and I do mean anyone, ever tells you that being the union representative is an honorable, important, and popular position, they should be tarred and feathered and run out of town on a rail. I am here to tell you the untold bitter truth of my tenure in 1982 as the National Football League Players Association team representative of the union members associated with the Dallas Cowboys Football Club.

I can honestly tell you that I survived that ordeal only because I didn't know that I was basically kept uninformed of the union leadership's plans. That fact, and the fact that my teammates believed I was, to a very great extent, uninformed of the union's direction during the strike, virtually absolved me in their eyes of any wrongdoing or disingenuousness pertaining to the conduct of the union.

That being said, I can unequivocally state that the troops led by my teammate and good buddy, Billy Joe DuPree, saved the game. I mean it. There was, with great certainty, no way the union had enough support of our constituents to approve any watered-down strike proposal that would have been presented by the NFLPA leadership. Not a prayer.

Today, the sports world believes that the union reached an agreement with the owners primarily and almost entirely through the efforts of an arbitrator. Nothing could be further from the truth.

For the most part, after reviewing the demands made by the union leadership, one finds that their demands were, shall we say, unreasonable and at best unrealistic. From the time I met with B. J. in training camp at Thousand Oaks (and throughout the remainder of preseason), the lack of accessibility of the leadership to the rank and file was, in his opinion, a huge mistake. He also believed that their inaccessibility and lack of openness created animosity and festered an increasing sense of distrust among the union membership. I agreed then, and I agree to a greater extent today.

Billy Joe would say to me, "House, what are these guys thinking? Don't they realize they are pissing off just about everybody? They talk to us in a condescending tone as if we don't understand what's going on. Like everyone in the union is a child. They act like they're our parents: 'Go to your room until we're done, and we will let you know what happened and what the new rules are.' Who do they think they are?"

Initially, the biggest issue of contention within the union was the leadership's desire to do away with individual representatives regarding individual player contract negotiations with each NFL team. That didn't sit well with virtually anyone.

My own determination regarding that issue was clearly defined and molded over the years of work I had done concerning contracts negotiations (both in business and as a football player). The attempt of the union leadership to use only representatives of the NFLPA to represent each NFL player with his particular employer was a severe conflict of interest, with zero chance of being approved by the union membership. It was an absurd and pathetic undertaking. It made the union leadership look incompetent and unsophisticated. How could the union leadership expect to equally represent the three Dallas Cowboys' tight ends (Doug Cosbie, B. J. DuPree, and Jay Saldi), for example, without a conflict of interest? They couldn't, and that was true with respect to every other position. There were many other scenarios throughout the entire league that made this intended undertaking by the NFLPA leadership absurd.

The fact that the NFLPA had to disband that idea during the early moments of the strike year showed a strong disregard for the union leadership by an overwhelming majority of its members. I clearly informed the leadership committee that my teammates were extremely disappointed that the leadership would even attempt to achieve such an openly unpopular request. I told them, as other player reps had, that the members considered it to be an act of conscious indifference to each individual player's value to his team. Although it appeared that the membership's disenchanted feelings were falling on deaf ears, the leadership quietly withdrew its resolution, requesting "the removal of individual player representatives" from its 1982 agenda platform.

Needless to say, the Ed Garvey, Gene Upshaw, Richard "Dick" Berthelsen, and Brig Owen leadership seemed undaunted and unaffected, despite the overwhelming fact that their union leadership's attempt to remove individual representation for each player by replacing those representatives with union reps was met head-on and dismantled by an overwhelming force of open rebellion and disapproval by the rank and file.

I have to admit, when looking back at what transpired, their arrogance was their undoing then, and it will probably be their undoing today.

During the summer of 1982, the union leadership traveled to each team's preseason training camp to address the players. It was clear by their presentation and agenda list that, although they sought the support of the union members, they spoke in a manner and tone as though they were somehow above it all. I'm sorry, let me correct myself: they spoke as if they were above it all and that they knew what was best for all of us.

I said to myself, *What a strange way to conduct yourself in seeking the support of your constituents.*

Let me put it this way: the leadership spent their time convincing the individual team player reps to remain onboard with their game plan, rather than convincing the overall membership. In reality, they had little or no legitimate game plan. They wanted the members to stand behind their version of a political regime. They wanted the player reps to keep the membership in line, that is, do it for them. It was as if they felt that if they could keep the player reps on their team, they could have smooth sailing in controlling the union as they saw fit. Upshaw and his colleagues knew that, in most cases, the most respected and trusted person on each team roster was the player rep. So, if they controlled the team player reps' support, they would control the union, indefinitely.

It was as if the union leadership ignored the fact that the union members were, in many cases, college graduates—people with their own thoughts and problems, unafraid to speak their minds in a huddle on the football field or on the playing field of life. Quite frankly, the union leadership underestimated the tenacity of each athlete—they were oblivious to or flat out ignored each athlete's desire to be treated fairly by both the owners and their union.

I recall a prevented altercation, or shall I say major confrontation, between several of my teammates and Gene Upshaw. While in Thousand Oaks, during the pre-season training camp in 1982, my teammates and I were retiring to our dorm rooms after meeting with the union leaders when a small group broke off to attempt to get some answers from Gene. I entered the housing area of Cal Lutheran and noticed Gene Upshaw distancing himself in a briskly paced, confident strut from the meeting area to the practice field parking lot. To my left, I observed Dupe (B. J. DuPree), Larry Bethea, Ron Springs, and Anthony Dickerson on a crash course that I estimated would have them converge with Gene a few strides from the cafeteria. With that, I turned back to my left and cut across the grassy knoll section just east of the dormitories. By cutting the distance between B. J.'s group and me in half, I was able to reach them just before they would get to Gene. Upshaw was within earshot of us, and they knew it. If Gene were to have continued his stroll, he would have had to go right past us. So, he waited. He was like a deer caught in a car's headlights.

I had to act quickly. I greeted the guys with a strong and confident voice: "What can I do for you guys? Do you have any other questions or issues you want to discuss so I can bring them to the next team rep committee meeting?" Acting as if I didn't want their response, I quickly added, "Because, if you do, can we first go get some pizza off campus before they close? I want to get off campus. I'm tired of the atmosphere around this place. It probably would make us all feel better anyway if we talked over some dinner."

When I finished my little diversionary tactic, I thought I had pulled it off. Unfortunately, B. J. would have none of it. He jumped right in and proceeded to cross-examine me.

"House, we know you're just trying to do your job, but Gene didn't try to answer or even deal with some issues that are of great concern to us. He acts like Garvey and his group know what's best for us and that we are just supposed to accept it without first knowing what they are intending to do or how they intend to do it. We were left hanging regarding some very important issues, and we want and need some answers."

With that, B. J. paused and glanced to his left to see if Upshaw would have the personal fortitude to address his banter. No, not Gene. He just stood there. He wanted no part of B. J. Not that day, not ever.

Dupe continued, "They've made promises before, remember? Remember?" He projected his voice toward Gene. "Because, if you don't remember, I am here to remind you that those promises weren't kept. The union and the owners put a spin on everything they did. House, that won't be the case this time. I promise you."

As B. J. waited for Gene to intervene (which I knew would never happen), I turned my broad, fire-hydrant body to the right (which would partially block Dupe's path to Upshaw). It was obvious that whatever I was about to say, it would have to be extremely convincing. I would have to be so convincing that it would curtail and defuse the elevated volatile feelings that existed until after the union leaders left the campus.

So, I made it personal.

"B. J.," I said softly, with as much of an engaging smile on my face as possible, "please don't do this on my watch. I don't want to be the only player rep to be unable to control his teammates. We've got to do things through channels. Every other team, including the Raiders, has agreed to go through their team representative to expedite matters and keep the communication lines equal and controllable. Could you imagine what chaos we would have if every player were allowed to contact the union leadership without having the restriction of going through a designated voice on each team? As much as we want to believe that each player would restrain himself, you and I both know better. That expectation would at best be improbable. So, work with me. Ask me the questions, and if I can't answer them adequately, I'll forward them to the committee—and I will do my best to get a satisfactory response back to you as quickly as I can."

"Nothing is gonna be any different. House, these guys are playing us just like the owners play us," B. J. said.

"B. J., this one time, humor me. Let me see what I can do. So, please tell me what questions you have. Okay?"

"All right," said B. J., "but listen up." He turned and pointed dramatically in Upshaw's direction. "He, that guy, clearly understands that the questions we want answered don't require research like rocket science. We want direct answers without any spin. We don't want there to be the possibility of any misconception; we want simple clear answers."

"I got what you mean," I replied softly, trying to be reassuring. But my problem was that the players didn't trust Ed Garvey, and they had little or no confidence in Upshaw or Berthelsen.

B. J. continued. "House, where is the strike fund they keep talking about, and what is the process that each player needs to follow in the event he needs to gain access to that fund? We asked in the meeting earlier this evening, and no one addressed it. They conveniently went off on a tangent, and the question was never answered. To this very day, we haven't received any semblance of an understandable answer about that strike fund. What's the answer? Do you know? Remember how Upshaw brought up the existence of the fund and how it would be available to help members during the strike period? Yet when he was asked about the details of the fund and the other questions pertaining to it, like being available to the members, Upshaw went off on something else. We want a detailed answer to that issue and those questions."

"I promise to get back with you this week when we do our joint workout," I said.

With that, B. J. paused for a moment and then with a certainty stated, "Robert,"—he always called me House, so that meant to me B. J. was being extra-serious—"the big three of this union leadership has little or no credibility with a great many of us. Believe me, I am not kidding. These guys are pushing the envelope with the members by conducting themselves in this holier-than-thou, know-it-all bullshit way. If they think I am overexaggerating, they are all in for one very rude awakening."

"Dupe, like I said before, I get where you are coming from. I promise to relay your concerns. When I get back from our next player rep meeting, I promise to get with you to discuss the status and tell you what I know."

"Fine. Let's go eat. I don't want to look at or talk about that S.O.B. anymore tonight. I want to enjoy that pizza. By the way, you're buying."

"No problem. Let's get outta here."

Unfortunately, B. J. ended up being right about those guys. It really was disheartening to see his concerns unfold into reality. But he was right, and thank God he didn't wait for them to irreparably screw it up.

As I look back, I clearly see how both the owners' and union leadership's arrogance would be a flaw that created a vital chink in their armor. Their sincere belief was that they each had a defense that could not be penetrated by their adversary or by the union rank and file. It also created an extremely high susceptibility for failure. Both the owners and the union higher echelon were vulnerable and ripe for virtual self-destruction. Unbeknownst to the owners and union leadership, they had just perfectly positioned themselves to face a reality their *power* could not overcome and their *arrogance* could no longer endure. Frankly, they would be humbled. And they deserved it.

CHAPTER 12
Inside Another Camp

A view from Fred Dean

I had been a member of the Washington Redskins roster since 1978; veteran players had been talking about the possibility of a strike for two years. Despite the tension, our training camp was one of unity and solidarity. This Redskins team was a close-knit group before training camp, during training camp, and during the season, and would continue to be unified during the strike. And though confidence in the union leadership was passive at best, we were still prepared to strike when the time presented itself. Soon, however, any positive feelings about the strike and union would dissolve. Luckily, my teammates would come to support my later decision to seek help for a different approach.

We were to play Philly and Tampa Bay before the season was to be interrupted by the strike. Even in the face of a nonseason, we were going to be ready to play these two games as if the championship were on the line; and when the strike started, we, as a team, chose to remain prepared. We had decided that we would practice, without coaches, every single day of the strike. Joe Theismann would get the plays so that if and when the season started again, we would have a well-rehearsed game plan. We had 100 percent participation. That harmony of spirit was what made our team so good.

We also had particularly strong team leaders that season. On offense, we had big John Riggins and our phenomenal quarterback Joe Theismann. Although Joe was making a lot of money, he was a team player; I don't think he was too thrilled about the guys who were running the union and how they were affecting his teammates. Our leaders on defense were Tony Peters and Monte Coleman. Dave Butz and Jeris White chipped in as leaders as well. George Starke, Joe Bostic, Joe Jacoby, Russ Grimm, Mark May, Ron Saul, and I were a shatterproof offensive line. We developed a common aggressiveness that was so obvious to the fans that we were tagged *The Hogs*, a nickname we proudly maintain today. George Starke, the head of the line, was labeled *Papa Hog*. At the time, we believed we were the best in football.

That year the Redskins were a very special group. As far as I am aware, the strike really took its toll on other teams; discontent was common throughout the league. But somehow we managed to stay tight in the face of it. Maybe that was because of what the strike could mean if successful. As the strike wore on, it was clear that our union leadership wasn't able to handle the owners. They were in over their heads. At meetings they would talk in circles and would never give a direct answer. When the strike became several weeks old, they even refused to return phone calls except through union team representatives. On top of this, they wanted all of us to allow union representatives to represent every player for individual employment contract negotiations. *No way!* we thought. *They are not going to replace my attorney.* I had been in the starting lineup since 1979 and took that responsibility very seriously. But I put my responsibility to my family ahead of anything. I simply knew that my mother wouldn't be too happy with that arrangement at all—that was for certain. People should ask that of themselves more often: *what would my mother think?*

As the strike went on into the sixth week, there was more tension between the players and the union leaders. I became extremely disappointed and upset with those union guys. They continued to blatantly withhold information and still would never give a full answer to a question. Even if they were holding out simply to avoid an angry response to the truth, their haziness backfired: few trusted them anymore. It hurt. The whole point of a union is to have an entity that can be counted on to do right by all its members; it seemed the NFLPA couldn't—or wouldn't—do right by us.

I had been talking with my friend and former coach Noel Brown for guidance. He told me what was going on with some of the players living in the Texas area. I soon spoke with those guys, and then I spoke with my friend and attorney Spence. As usual, he had thoroughly analyzed the problem and had come up with a way to end this stuff.

Right around the seventh week, the team decided to take a few days to a week off because we had been practicing every day. I traveled to my off-season home in Houston. While I was there, Spencer had a "problem" with some people, and Noel called to tell me. So, I went to Dallas to back up Spence. But a trip to Dallas was no reason to quit conditioning. One of my teammates joined me later that week to work out. We practiced every day for about two and a half hours, just like the rest of the team had continued to do. There was a school near Spence's house, and I would go there to run. I used Spence's pool to keep up aerobic conditioning. No one would accuse my teammates or me of slacking off.

The time approached for us to execute our plan. The only thing that bothered me was that because of the way it would get done, no one would know that the union and the owners would be forced into a position to settle by a small group of us players. The country would be under the impression that the union leadership *was* doing what they were supposed to do for us. But Spence made us realize that doing what we were doing wasn't about ego—it was about results. We were sure of what we had to do and had the group to get it done. And now, finally, the truth will be out.

CHAPTER 13
Golf with B. J. and Rayfield

A view from Spencer Kopf

The telephone rang, interrupting my descent into a dining room chair. I picked up the phone and on the other end was this deep, calm voice that said, "Spence, B. J. DuPree."

"Hey, B. J. What's up? You okay?"

"Sure, everything is as good as could be expected. Look, Rayfield and I have a tee time tomorrow, and I thought you would come if I twisted your arm. Plus, I would like to go over some business with you, and I couldn't think of a better setting."

I paused for a moment. I checked my calendar, which happened to be sitting to my right on the dining room table. I had no scheduled settings at any of the local courts, and my earliest booked appointment was at 2:00 p.m. The only pressing matter on my agenda was a time I had set aside for the wedding caterer. I had already missed two meetings and was certain to be toast if I missed this one. But golf, that's a different priority.

"Consider my arm twisted. What time and where?"

"L. B. Houston at 9:00 a.m. Let's get breakfast at 7:30 a.m. and then hit some range balls before we play," said B. J.

"Fine. See you then."

———————————

The next day ...

It was a beautiful Tuesday morning. There was very little breeze, and it was comfortably warm. Rayfield Wright arrived just before tee time looking like he had never left professional football. He stood slightly more than six and a half feet and weighed around 270 pounds. He didn't have an ounce of disproportionate fat on his body. He was a pure athlete who had originally played tight end, but was converted to offensive tackle by the Dallas Cowboys. He became arguably the greatest player at this position in the history of the NFL. Ray was named First Team All Decade for the 1970s and was later inducted into the Hall of Fame. His smile could light up a room, and he was a man of principles. In 1974 he signed a future contract, along with Larry Csonka, to play in the World Football League (WFL), seeking better remuneration for his talent as a football player. Players would follow suit nearly ten years later with the formation of the USFL spring football league. (Unlike the WFL, the USFL had a television contract.) Rayfield had no trouble speaking his mind and backing up his convictions with reason and action.

Billy Joe was on the driving range when I arrived. He had a pure, fluid golf swing, which was extremely rare for a man of his height. "Dupe," as he was referred to by his teammates, was a strong yet quiet man who let his actions on the football field do his talking. He was the first-round pick of the Dallas Cowboys in 1973 out of Michigan State University, just as Larry Bethea had been in 1978. While in college, B. J., a political science student, and other athletes from the football, basketball, and soccer teams formed the Coalition of Black Athletes to protest the Big Ten Conference not having black referees for Big Ten Conference games. They boycotted the games until the Big Ten relented and assigned black officials to ref. He was the consummate leader by example, and when he spoke it was like watching an old E. F. Hutton television commercial; everyone stopped what he or she was doing to hear what Billy Joe DuPree had to say.

Here I was, all of five-foot-seven (depending on what shoes I was wearing), standing on the first tee between these two gentle giants. Just imagine how that looked to the starter, who announced the "on deck" threesome. Funny as that may seem, however, I fully intended to whip their butts. But apparently golf was not the main agenda of the day. B. J. was not the type to jump into a discussion when he had a serious matter on his mind; he tended to brood and think things over first. B. J. said nothing at the driving range and nothing of substance until the third hole (a short par four dogleg to the right over a line of tall trees).

"Spence, this upcoming strike … you see, I read your article in the *News*, and everything you said was right on the money. The problem, as I see it, is that the union leadership doesn't have a clue where they are going or what to do when they get there. The guys are grossly unprepared for a strike, especially if it becomes long. They also have no confidence in Garvey—I know I don't. Also, I think the owners know that and are waiting for the union to self-destruct. Can we players protect ourselves from the path the union is taking? Is there anything we can do? I'm in my tenth year, and I don't have many seasons left. What can we do to help ourselves? Tell me."

After completing his oration, B. J. promptly took out his three wood, crushed his drive over the trees, cutting the dogleg, and his ball landed on the green forty-five feet from the pin. He strolled back to the golf cart and said with his silence, *Spence, you have the rest of the hole to contemplate your answer.* I wondered what he would have done to the ball had it pissed him off.

I contemplated for a moment as Rayfield took out his two iron (he wouldn't use a wood all day) and cut the dogleg as well, his ball landing some sixty yards in front of the green in the short grass.

My turn. I took out my four iron and landed near the middle of the fairway, approximately 130 yards from the hole. I hit my second shot to about twenty feet away and two-putted for par. Rayfield struck an awesome wedge to four feet and sank his birdie. Ironically, Dupe, who drove the green, three-putted for par. He wasn't very pleased. When Rayfield said, "Now there is a perfect example that you drive for show and you putt for dough," it didn't sit very well with B. J. at first. It was said all in good fun, but I'm glad it wasn't me who had teased.

We reached the fourth hole, and B. J. gently pressed me for a solution to his concerns. I had contemplated my response, gathered my thoughts, and said, "I do have an idea to equal the playing field with the owners. But, first I need to research and discuss certain procedural issues and confirm certain facts with some buddies of mine concerning the union and its conduct. Then, I need to analyze an issue that is pertinent only as it pertains to the owners. I'll let you know by the end of the week what can be done, if anything."

"Okay by me," B. J. said. "Just let me know as soon as you know, and when you can start, okay?"

"Whoa! Wait a minute, kemo sabe!" I yelled. "I just said I'd let you know how you could go about it, if at all, not that I would do it."

"Look, Spence. Just let me know something soon. We can't sit by and let them ruin our lives just because they think they can. I have a family that's relying on me. I can tell you this: I can't sit by and do nothing. Our player reps are informed only to a certain extent. They really don't sit in on the process and certainly don't have a strong voice with the people running things. It's frustrating and frightening for me, both as a player and a family man. Please look at it and get back to me soon. We'll talk to some of the guys like Norm, Don, Doug, Springs, and Larry, and I'll get back with you Sunday evening. Okay?"

"All right," I said. "We'll talk Sunday. Now, you'd better concentrate. No excuses."

"Let's double the bet if you think I need to concentrate to beat your sorry butt."

Let's just say, outside the results on the scorecard, the real score was how tight our friendship has grown since that golf outing. Such friendships are rare, and I am extremely fortunate to have a friend of that caliber.

Sunday evening ...

When we met, I gave B. J. the response he was hoping for. I didn't just placate or please him: we had come up with an actual solution that, based on the way certain circumstances unfolded, had a better than reasonable chance of success. Because of the apparent stubbornness, greed, and lust for control of "their game," the owners had exposed themselves. And the arrogance and poorly developed plan and direction of the union leadership had, in turn, exposed them. If the scenario ran as expected, our strategy, if timely implemented, would probably succeed. It seemed incredible, but it was accurate.

I explained it something like this: "Guys, it will take some shrewd maneuvering, both legally and personally; however, if we all conduct ourselves in a maverick, unshakable way—with the appearance that we care only for justice, that the consequences are irrelevant—the owners and the union leadership should capitulate and make peace. That's it. There is no other way. The sole issue of this strike is who is in control. If we take control, we could jeopardize the entire season, and they'll make peace. No one wins, but no one loses and no one loses face. But the players have *nothing* to lose the way things are, and the owners and union have *everything* to lose. All we need to do is arrange it so that the owners and the union realize our position, as well as the one we put them in."

Anthony Dickerson, Fred Dean, and Norm Wells said in succession: "I agree."

Then B. J. responded, "Let's get as many guys as we can trust and set up a time to meet. Spence, thanks for your time. We'll get in touch with Noel to set it up."

Anthony Dickerson: Linebacker, ladies' man

All-Pro Billy Joe DuPree...

Doug Cosbie, Shirley (Spence's mother), and Larry Bethea

Danny Spradlin and Spence – "We won!"

Dave and Spencer talk about the win.

Don and Spence ask, "How do we top this?"

Don Smerek

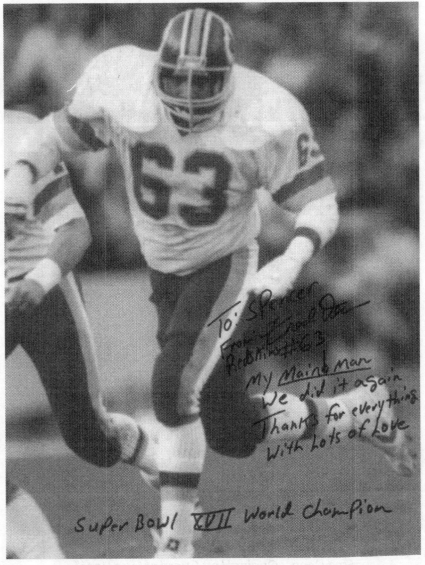

Fred Dean in action

Fred Dean – Original Left Guard of "The Hogs"

*John Fitzgerald and
Norm Wells holding up
Spence at the wedding*

Billy Joe and Marsha

Joe DeLamielleure

Joe DeLamielleure in action

Joe slightly angry

Sworn in and ready to work

Larry and Spence – best buds

Lisa, Spence and Don right after the settlement's confirmation

*Noel, Spence, Fred Nelson (Kansas City Chiefs),
David Barrett (Tampa Bay Buccaneers)*

Norm Wells

Norm Wells, former United States Attorney of the Northern District of Texas Jim Rolfe, and Spence celebrate.

Robert Newhouse in action . . .

Scott Murray, 1982

Scott Murray, 2009

Allen judge named to he

By K.C. SWAN
Staff Writer

PLANO — The Collin County Public Officials Association held its annual spring banquet Friday evening in Plano. During the proceedings, Allen Municipal Judge Spencer Kopf was sworn in as president of the Texas Municipal Courts Association by Judge Joe Draughn, 14th District Court of Appeals, Houston.

Judge Draughn also announced Judge Kopf's nomination for a seat on the Texas Judicial Review Commission. The nomination came from the Texas Supreme Court and Judge Kopf is one of three Texas municipal judges to be nominated.

According to Judge Draughn, this is the first time that a municipal judge has been nominated for the high honor. Judge Kopf is the first municipal judge from North Texas to be elected as the municipal courts association's president and the youngest member to be elected to the office.

Judge Joe L. Draughn, 14th District Court of Appeals, Houston gives the oath of office to Judge Spencer Kopf (pictured at right) Friday night at the Collin County Public Officials spring banquet. Judge Kopf was sworn in as president of the Texas Municipal Courts Association and nominated for the Texas Judicial Review Commission. (Staff photo).

ead state group

"I share this achievement with the City of Allen," Kopf said after the swearing-in ceremonies. "I will do my best to make you proud."

Judge Kopf has served as municipal judge in Allen for two and a half years and is known for his achievements as a "sports" lawyer. Several of his clients include members of the Dallas Cowboys.

The guest speaker for the association's banquet was Texas Public Utilities Commission Commissioner Dennis Thomas. Thomas has served on the PUC since August, 1984 and is the former deputy executive assistant to Govenor Mark White.

In his address to the 200-plus group, Thomas discussed the PUC's Friday decision concerning the emergency stay on payments of General Telephone foreign-exchange (FX) service bills.

The PUC is expected to call a public hearing in Austin within the next two weeks to discuss the new billing structure that has resulted in large increases in FX customer's bills.

Thomas discussed the functions and duties of the PUC as a regulatory agency, addressing key issues such as phone service and utilities.

The commissioner explained that the PUC has two goals in the area of telephone service: state-of-the-art service and universally affordable phones.

"We have made a lot of changes," he said, referring to PUC rulings concerning telephone service after the break-up of AT&T. "But you will see a lot more."

Areas Thomas targeted for change include computer "smart buildings" and coin phones. Concerning electricity, Thomas touched on the point that it is "an increasing marginal cost industry — the more you build the more it will cost."

He explained that when dealing with utilities, there exists a regulatory technology that does not fit the industry.

Spence is sworn in.

Spence and Don Smerek celebrating

Spencer and Judge Ron Chapman talking shop

One on one with Willis Reed

Jerri Mote and Tex Schramm

*Jerri Mote – the Cowboys'
Miss Reliable*

Tony Davis, 2010

"Tough" Tony Davis in action

Barry Horn: 2009 Texas Sports Writer of the Year

CHAPTER 14
The Players Seek a Meeting

A view from Spencer Kopf, two days later

The second Monday into the strike, I received a call from Noel and Fred that several players (active and inactive) living in and visiting the Texas area had requested a meeting. Because I was busy handling other office matters, I instructed Lisa to coordinate with Noel to facilitate the request. She made an accurate count of the players expected to attend. The group was going to be large, so Noel suggested that we get refreshments. I instructed Noel to direct the players to the rear entrance of the office, away from the main lobby; that way, we could at least *attempt* to avoid making a scene.

By then I had spoken at length with Billy Joe DuPree, Anthony Dickerson, and Fred Dean about the purpose of the meeting and the goals the players were seeking to achieve. B. J. told me to reiterate my thoughts from my July 11 column and to address any questions the players had regarding the strike *before* sharing any theory for a solution. His instruction was shrewd: only a few players are as savvy as B. J., and so a restatement of the boondoggle was important to be sure everyone was on the same page. I decided further to make it perfectly clear that I would actually represent only a specific few; but if other players wished to attend the meeting, that would be acceptable to me—that is, as long as they could maintain their taciturnity about the details.

Expressway Tower was located at the southeast corner at the intersection of Yale Boulevard and the northbound service road of North Central Expressway. The second floor of the building extended outward from its north side, which was the space occupied by the Dallas version of Hugh Hefner's Playboy Club. (My barber was also located on the second floor, and since he's been gone, I haven't had a truly decent haircut.) At approximately 9:30 on Thursday morning, a small motorcade arrived at the southern parking lot. The men entered through the side doors and congregated in the lobby that was the closest to the elevators. It appeared to be a scene right out of *Gulliver's Travels*, but that day about *thirty* Gullivers had set foot in Lilliput. Several of the guys commented that discretion was virtually impossible. The unassuming citizens in the lobby stood awed as this throng of behemoths awaited the opening of the elevator doors. Several members of the media had gotten word somehow and had entered the building ahead of the players. Ironically, none of them had the temerity to question even one player as to why they were there. Based upon the cantankerous expressions on some of the players' faces, that was probably a wise tack to take.

The players filled a few of the elevator cars and traveled to the fifth floor, where they were greeted by Noel. He escorted them down the long westward hallway until they reached the next-to-last door on the right. They entered the waiting area outside of Noel's office and were led into a well-furnished conference area adorned with assorted pastries, bagels, coffee, and other refreshments. We allowed them to visit with each other while they partook of the buffet, so that they could relieve tension for the anticipated conference. (Two points for Lisa and Noel.) Presently the players eased their way into my private office, which surprisingly housed them all quite comfortably. There were only a few places to sit, but it was clear that this meeting was intended to be concise.

Initially, based upon the conversations among the players, the main problem and concern would be keeping our thoughts and strategies to ourselves. We had to create an arrangement with all the men that they would cooperate and support the group action in a united front. Our adversaries had to believe that we were adamant in our resolve regardless of the outcome. B. J. addressed the players in a very calm, quiet tone, with a unique, firm delivery that he had honed to perfection in many a huddle. It went something like this:

> We are all here today to air our concerns and our opinions regarding the strike. We have decided to seek a direction as a group with the assistance of counsel. We are here to determine if there is anything that we can do to create a disturbance that will be large enough to instigate a settlement in these so-called "labor talks."
>
> Now, I have talked at length with Spence, and he has developed several avenues to approach these issues. He has the assistance of some talented legal minds and sideline coaching from some undercover members of the press.
>
> However, it will require our cooperation and devotion to the scheme if it is to be successful. Remember, we will only be

as strong as our weakest link. There cannot be—we cannot have—a weak link. There can be no leaks as to what Spence is preparing to do or how, when, or where he is going to do it. No one is to know outside of this room. Not wives, not loved ones, not family members, not clergy, not anyone. Absolutely no one. If you have any questions about what our little group is doing, contact Noel or me.

If you care about having a chance to win, please keep what we are doing private. We are sharing this with you guys today because we feel you should look at the choices and realize that we must do what we are doing. We are a small group and felt we should share what we are doing with certain friends. If you want to support us—great. If not, please keep it to yourself. If you don't think you can do that, we must ask you to leave.

Let me say this: if we back this play, and our assessment of the owners and the union leadership is inaccurate, we will be no worse off than we are at this very moment. However, if we are correct, we will better ourselves and the chances of others who follow us.

We gathered you together because numbers mean strength. Since a lot of you are not employed by my team, it will most certainly generate curiosity among the owners and the union leadership. You saw the press in the lobby as we entered the building. They know, at least for this morning, we weren't here to see my boss, and it's too early to go visit the bunnies.

Unless there are some really pressing questions, I would like Spence to address all of us as a group as to why we are here and why, despite the apparent Goliaths we have for opponents, we have a significant chance of being successful. Spence ...

And I said:

If you read the article I submitted to the Dallas Morning News, *at the paper's request I might add, you will see that, so far, we all have a pretty good grasp of what is occurring in this strike and why. If you look clearly at the conduct of both sides, it is and will be obvious that there is one major weakness between them. Our team sincerely believes that the weakness that the owners and the players share will, quite frankly, cause them—in fact, force them—to seek peace with each other. That weakness may even force the owners to do something that they truly do not consciously believe they will ever do: provide additional compensation to you players.*

We believe that this union leadership will not effect significant changes to the current collective bargaining agreement. They have poorly planned this strike. Only until the courts determine the right for each and every one of you to seek employment where you desire, will you be able to make those significant strides for personal basic benefits.

At this time, you are being guided by a union leadership in which you have zero confidence; you are employed by ownership that you all believe is consciously indifferent to your well-being and that of your families. Therefore, if I am to risk life and limb to deal with these two bullies, I need and expect complete solidarity among those who participate. None of you can waver. Timing and complete cooperation is essential, if not crucial, to our having a chance. Are we agreed? [All responded affirmatively.] *Good.*

At this time, I cannot share exactly what I intend to do until the time to do it arrives. But when that time presents itself, you will be notified. You will be counted on just as if you were blocking for your quarterback who needs time to throw the bomb to a wide-open, sure-handed receiver.

B. J. stuck up both his arms, and everyone laughed.

I continued, "Are we agreed?" Again, everyone responded affirmatively. "Excellent. Now, are there any questions?"

Anthony Dickerson said, "Yes. Tell them the cost if it is done right."

And I wrapped it up:

If you gentlemen will do what we need you to do when we need you to do it, it will cost nothing because the strike will resolve itself. But when it's time to step up, you will need to put on your game faces and be ready to play. If you decide to support these guys, you must be behind me like the Hebrews behind Moses on the way out of Egypt. These people have to sense your resolve. They must believe we are mavericks—that we are going to stand up for ourselves because no one else will and because justice is worth defending at all costs. You follow me?

Okay. Now, if you fellas will excuse me, I think it's time for me to go—I have wedding plans to deal with....

Tony: How'd this stay under wraps? I mean, how the hell did this not leak out?

Joe: It'll be out ... soon.

Tony: Yeah, I get that, but come on. No one noticed back then?

Joe: Oh, people noticed.... Tell him, B. J.

Billy Joe: Yeah, Tex Schramm, one of the higher guys on the NFL management team, was there, in the same building as Spence's office. He knew. How couldn't he? He heard about all of us showing up, and Spence knew it, too. He wanted to see what Tex would say to him.

Tony: Was he pissed?

Billy Joe: Concerned's more like it. He knew Spence well, and knew if Spence was involved, it had to be legal, and it had to be serious....

CHAPTER 15
Tex Seeks a Meeting

A view from Spencer Kopf

I had just returned from court, having appeared before Judge Harold Entz. I quickly visited with him, his bailiff Sam Reese, and his Court Coordinator Greg Shumpert, and headed back to the office. Just as I was approaching my desk, Lisa buzzed me—I had a call on line two that seemed important. I first picked up the phone and asked her who it was, and she replied, "It's Jerri Mote from the Cowboys'." I abruptly told her to have Don come to my office immediately, to hold all calls, and to tell Miss Mote that I would be with her shortly.

Don walked in, and I asked him, "Has the earth split in two—have there been any earthquake warnings emanating from under our building?"

He replied, not annoyed, but not amused, "No—why?"

"Because, kemo sabe, Tex Schramm wants to talk."

Don shrugged it off, saying, "Who did you expect to hear from after thirty football players from different teams are in your office at the same time, the Easter Bunny? Just pick up the phone and find out what he wants. Then decide if you're going to move to Australia...."

After taking several slow, deep breaths, I lifted the phone and pushed the line-two button, and said, "Hello" (but it felt like *Start your engines*).

Jerri said, in her professional, not-quite-monotone voice, "Good morning, Spencer. Mr. Schramm has asked me to see if you were available to meet with him. I am sorry for the short notice, but this just came up. He said he would appreciate the courtesy."

I asked her, "When does he want to meet?"

"Now would be great. As you know, we are on eleven. I'll meet you at the receptionist's desk. I realize this is very spur-of-the-moment, but he is anxious to speak with you before he leaves for some other meetings." Boy, she was good at her job.

"Let me clear one matter, and I'll be up in, say, fifteen minutes," I said.

"I'll tell Mr. Schramm. Thanks, Spencer."

It was her job to get me up there before I tried to reach him on the telephone. I'm no Sherlock Holmes, but that spoke volumes to me—and to Don, too. It was clear that he wanted to make sure that whatever was to be said between us that day was free from any risk of being documented by any press or tape recorder.

Don suggested a quick powwow before I went into the lion's den. He thought that it might be better, from a psychological standpoint, to seek a delay in the meeting. While I agreed with Don's analysis, I had a feeling that the timing of Tex's request, coupled with his sense of urgency, was a sign of confusion—and we needed all of the advantages we could get. I instructed Lisa to call Cathy and tell her I would be late for our lunch appointment.

As I started out the door, Lisa called to me, "Good luck! You sure you don't want to take Noel along?"

I reached the eleventh floor, which was wholly occupied by the Dallas Cowboys' organization; the receptionist greeted me. She had been informed of my impending arrival. She greeted me warmly and then, over the intercom, told Jerri that I was in the lobby. As I waited for Jerri, Coach Landry approached the elevator with his secretary, Barb Goodman. They both smiled, and Coach Landry asked, "How did the U. S. Attorney like his football?"

I had requested a personal autographed football from Coach Landry to give as a gift to my friend for his investiture as the United States Attorney for the Northern District of Texas. I said, "He has it displayed in one of the more prominent spots in his office. He was overwhelmed by your personal sentiment. It went over huge— thanks, Coach."

"I enjoyed doing it, Spence. Anytime," he said as he and Barb stepped into the elevator.

I had worked hard to establish a level of respect with Coach Landry over the years. I made sure that his confidence in me never wavered. Coach and I would meet from time to time to discuss the players and the shuffle that was the sports industry. Our relationship, it seemed to me, was unceremonious—a collection of cordial, respectful exchanges. But he eventually directed Buck Buchanan, the equipment manager for the team, to grant me access to the practice facilities at Forest and Abrams to meet with players and assist them on their legal matters. All of the coaches knew me and seemed pleased to see me whenever I happened to stop by; as far as I know, no other legal representative had ever been granted that continuous privilege.

At a lunch I had with Barb Goodman and Doug Todd at the Cowboy offices, Barb made it clear that I enjoyed a special relationship with Coach that others didn't. He was especially proud of me when I was first appointed to the municipal bench, and then even more so when he learned of my election as president of the Texas Municipal Courts Association. I was always straight and direct with Coach Landry, and so was he with me. He knew he could rely on what I said; he knew he could rely on me. For Coach Landry and the Dallas Cowboys, that would be significant in the upcoming weeks of the strike and during the heart of the USFL/NFL bidding war for player contracts.

Most attorneys, I'm sure, expect a sense of nervous anticipation in preparing for a case before the court. I expect the nerves. But I was unusually calm and was confident in my resolve to learn as much as I could from Tex without tipping my hand. Like Fast Eddie Felson, I felt tight but good. I guess I was just extremely curious as to what was transpiring beneath the surface; so I told myself to relax and let him talk—let him control the room, so he's comfortable. *Observe his body language, Spence.*

Tex Schramm was not a striking figure. But he was extremely successful in portraying a presence of being a man who expected to control a meeting, and he usually accomplished just that. He spoke quite slowly and concisely, with small, occasional sharp gestures— his little exclamation points. These mannerisms fit a man who was used to being listened to. That was fine with me. I was here to gain information, not to debate. I realized that if I did speak, I needed to be terse.

Tex was on the telephone as I was escorted into his office. He motioned for me to sit, which I did. The whole scene appeared choreographed: under normal circumstances, I would wait opposite Jerri Mote's desk until his telephone call was completed. Instead, I sat waiting for him to conclude his conversation. *Just shut up and listen, Spence.*

Tex finished his call and immediately greeted me before he had placed the receiver down in the cradle. "Spencer, thank you for interrupting your day to meet with me. I have to tell you that even though I haven't had a chance to tell you personally, we are all impressed and pleased with how Mike Hegman has turned around. You've done a great job for him and for some other guys on the team as well. I realize that some of their stuff could have been pretty bad. What I'm saying is, we really appreciate the manner in which you handle your business. Keeping the players' business and problems quiet benefits everyone, especially them. That speaks volumes to us up here."

Then, abruptly, the throat clearing ended, and Tex immediately cut to the chase and asked, "But, tell me this, why would over thirty players meet with you early in the morning? That entourage created quite a stir in this building." He spoke as if he was quietly berating a child. His insistent curiosity seemed to fill the room with every breath he took.

"Tex, you know I can't divulge any contents of a meeting I have had with a client or even a potential client. All I will say is that I was providing my legal expertise."

Tex went into a willful, passionate denunciation of the union's unrealistic, overzealous, and unjustified stance. He unrealistically believed that he could sway an adversary despite the issues or the stakes. That was also the apparent stance of the majority of the owners, but not all. Tex proceeded to quote from the article I had written for the *Dallas Morning News* regarding the NFLPA and its "PATCO-like demands."

"This whole thing is just unreasonable and unjustified," he said. His tirade, while volume-controlled, continued uninterrupted for some fifteen minutes. When he concluded, he solicited my response to his perception of the strike, its issues, and the union leadership.

I began with a terse reiteration of my position on the NFLPA's conduct, consistent with the July 11 article. The time was not right to divulge the intense distrust and uneasiness my clients had toward the leadership of the union. But I did assert that my clients were totally justified in their dissatisfaction with the position that the owners had taken. I appreciated his passion, I said, but found his position totally unsupported by the facts.

I continued (so much for concision), "On February 23, all of the salaries of your team were published and discussed on the front page of the *Dallas Morning News*. Since then, I have gained access to the terms and conditions of those contracts. All of them. In fact, I have gotten them for the entire league. Do you really want to spend time trying to change my perspective regarding the 'reasonable compensation issue' of player contracts? From a business and legal perspective, especially in light of the over two-billion-dollar television contract signed by the league, those salaries and bonus packages are absurd. Plus, in the face of that overwhelming evidence, it sure doesn't help matters or endear the players to your position when someone on your staff states, 'If you asked 100 players if they were underpaid, 99 would say they are.'"

He just stared, so I continued, "I believe I have made it crystal clear that the union is not acting in the overall best interest of all the players. That, coupled with the inadequate compensation, lack of satisfactory health benefits, pension funding, and restricted employment, totally justifies whatever action any players decide to take. Believe me."

He sat up from the leaned-back position he had originally taken and pulled his chair close to his desk. He looked directly into my eyes.

I said, "Technically, the players are entertainers with unique talent ... and a short life span. Their work is violent, which also makes their employment tenuous. I don't disagree with you that the union is seeking too much in this particular labor negotiation. I definitely believe that the owners are being a little self-destructive. The owners group is like a kid who, if he can't play quarterback or run the game the way he wants it played, just might take his football and go home. So, I say, be careful of what you demand because you just may get it.

"Look, Tex, these players don't have adequate health coverage. They are *grossly* underpaid and are being denied the right to protect themselves. I realize that the owners will never freely or voluntarily submit to free agency; but you know and I know that when the issue of free agency is heard by the courts, the owners will eventually succumb."

"What is it you're saying, then?" Tex asked.

"If you want to buy more time," I said, "you'll delay the inevitable and probably bring an end to this childish standoff. It will require remuneration for the time missed and adequate salary increases and bonuses based on years in the league, position played, playing time, and overall value to the team. It must be similar to what was previously discussed at our last meeting about this very same subject matter. Otherwise—well, I'm no soothsayer, but I *can* add two plus two. Now, besides that, do you remember offensive lineman Norm Wells? Remember *him*?"

What happened to Norm Wells ...

Norm Wells was a graduate of Northwestern University. He was a handsome, articulate offensive lineman and one of the strongest members of the Dallas Cowboys' roster. He stood six feet, six inches and was approximately 285 pounds. Norm had blown out his knee in 1980 and had season-ending major surgery. He was preparing to report to camp and attempt to play on one leg. At the office, with his fiancée present, he sought advice on what he could do legally to protect his interests.

At that time, no player had ever challenged the opinion of the team doctors, even when it came to performing surgery. I advised Norm to go to Oklahoma City and get examined by Dr. Donald O'Donohue, a foremost authority on orthopedic surgery. He had operated on Gale Sayers, Dick Butkus, and Willis Reed, former NBA MVP. Norm was thoroughly examined by Dr. O'Donohue, who informed Norm that his playing days were over. The doctor wrote a thorough medical opinion for my use.

Naturally, Norm took it hard because his heart still wanted to play. He insisted that he had at least a year left in him. I called the doctor and requested that he revisit his diagnosis with Norm—this time, with a sense of firmness that Norm would be unable to ignore. I didn't hear the conversation between Norm and the doctor. Neither one of them shared the contents of that telephone call. Norm called and told me he was now ready for training camp.

Norm Wells reports to training camp ...

Norm was worried how he would handle himself when he arrived at the practice fields. The team doctor had issued him a special knee brace. Norm was certain they would pass him when he took his physical; I was sure that after he was there a week or two, they would certainly cut him from the roster, claiming he could not outplay the new recruits. Norm shared with me what happened at training camp that day:

> *Just as expected, the team doctor gave me the physical with the special brace they provided. At the conclusion of the medical examination, the doctor approached me with a smile and said, "Congratulations, your knee has responded well to rehab. You've passed."*
>
> *I excused myself and called Dallas for reassurance and then called Spence to review what I would do next. After concluding our telephone conference, I sucked up all the self-esteem I could muster and slowly walked the campus of Cal Lutheran before seeking an audience with Coach Landry.*
>
> *As I approached Coach Landry, my heart was racing faster than when I was just ready to take the field in a Big Ten football game. Coach Landry seemed larger than life to most of us. But today I was making a family decision, and that responsibility quickly cured any anxiety I was feeling. I excused myself for the interruption in his schedule and said, "Coach, I have something I need to give you. It's real important."*
>
> *"What is it, Norm?" he asked.*
>
> *"It's a medical evaluation by Dr. O'Donohue of Oklahoma City. You see, Coach, I have been having a hard time rehabbing,*

and I knew when we were getting ready to come to camp, my knee might not be ready. I still wanted to give it all I had, as always. But I couldn't get it to respond. So, I sought out another medical opinion to see if something was wrong, because I was being told it should be okay. You'll see by this report, it's pretty bad. Spencer Kopf, my attorney, told me you would understand. The doctor said that I had no choice—that I had a football-related injury that needed additional, extensive repair; otherwise, my career would be over. He said he would talk to the team to explain his reasoning. I really wanted to give it a go, but I have to protect my family. My doctor said he would talk with whomever you wanted."

As I finished, a peace came over me. I couldn't believe I was able to do it.

Thirty minutes later, I was called into Coach Landry's office, where Coach advised me that the team physician had reevaluated my knee; and despite my passing the physical, he had determined that without additional surgery and rehab, the knee would be unable to withstand the rigors of playing football at the highest level. He thanked me for my tenacity and hard work ethic and told me I would remain on the team; however, I was to be placed on injured reserve. At a minimum, I had just added one and a half years to my career because I had challenged the sports medicine tradition, which had never been confronted in the history of the Cowboys.

But my career had been cut drastically short. After that meeting, I played only one more down as a professional football player before reinjuring my knee. But had Spence not had me see O'Donohue and issue a challenge to the team's doctors, I would have been cut from the team and out of a job and money.

Those short eighteen months went by quickly. I remember the last day. My eyes swelled up with tears. My football days were over. I strolled down the path leading away from the building housing the Dallas Cowboys' management and coaches, and my tears turned to tears of joy: I had just made over ninety thousand dollars for swallowing my pride and standing up for myself in a manner that no one had done before. Other teammates would soon follow my example. I am very proud of that. Big time.

Back to Tex's office ...

"Tex," I said, "if the Dallas Cowboys' physical stands and Norm Wells is cut later because he's unable to beat out other players, he gets nothing from the team from that point forward; if, however, Norm Wells fails the team physical based on injuries that occurred during the previous regular season, then he would be entitled to 100 percent of his 1982 regular season salary plus half of the 1983 regular season salary. In our present situation, there is a lot that needs to be addressed, and these players won't back off. Obviously, fair pay and medical benefits are the main issues. Whether or not the union is able to focus on those basic issues with you guys is the story of the day."

"It seems quite apparent that you are not working for the NFLPA," he said. "You certainly are not working for us. And it's now quite clear that you and your clients intend to beat to your own drummer. So, if you decide to do any interviews for the papers, radio, television, or any legal processes, I'd appreciate a heads-up."

"That request is a little premature. But I will notify my clients at the appropriate time. That's the best I can do for now," I said.

He now knew that my clients were so nonconformist that the owners and the union would be unable to dissuade or control them. Worse, the owners would be unable to speculate our intentions. But I had also presented the truth to Tex: he was aware of the issues and the steps we were willing to take. We could no longer be ignored.

I called Don at Caulfield's Restaurant and reported the news.

CHAPTER 16
The Owners' Huddle

A view from Spencer Kopf

As I was leaving the confines of Jerri Mote's desk, I overheard Tex buzz and ask her to set up a conference call with the strike committee and to bring him the file on Norm Wells. He directed Jerri to order lunch in and asked her to cancel his lunch date and first afternoon meeting.

The following is a synopsis of the conference call based upon information gathered and relayed to me by one party to the call and two former Dallas Cowboys' staff members who were privy to the contents of the conversation.

By the time the multiple-party call had been arranged, the food had arrived for Tex, but it remained untouched. Tex had already tried to reach Coach Landry, but Landry had not yet returned to the office. Tex summoned Don Wilson, the Chief Financial Officer, into his office and instructed Jerri to hold all calls.

The first person came on the line. Tex started the conversation: "We might have an unexpected problem with this strike crap." Just as he was about to continue, the operator interrupted and advised Tex that his second party was being patched in. "Hello, gentlemen, what's up?" the new voice uttered. Tex continued, "I was just saying that we might have a real fly in the ointment here in Dallas regarding this strike stuff."

"Go on," said caller one.

"It could be nothing—and, then again, it might become a mess. You guys remember that article I sent you from the *Dallas Morning News* about the ineptness of the NFLPA leadership? Well, the attorney who wrote that article has just been visited by over thirty players, active and retired, to review the legal issues of the strike."

"I've seen it, but I haven't read it yet," said caller one.

"Well, read it," Tex exhorted. "This guy blasts the union leadership good, and then some."

"Well, then, what seems to be the problem?" asked caller one.

"This guy wrote the article as a favor to Dave Smith. I met with him today—the attorney. I'll tell you this: he doesn't respect the leadership qualities of Garvey one bit ..."

Caller one interrupted: "Well, that doesn't sound like much of a problem. He can't do anything to interfere with this process. Look, he's one man with a group of upset players. Anyway, if his problem is with the union, how does that affect us?"

Tex interjected, "His opinion of *our* position on this strike is far from flattering. He knows the issues and is pretty blunt about how they should be resolved. If he had the proper situation, he would be addressing free agency in a federal court tomorrow. Frankly, the article he wrote is pretty precise. And the press is going to eat up his use of our TV contract to support his argument that the players are grossly underpaid. He said the lack of proper medical benefits for men who risk their health by engaging in such violent work is both 'appalling' and 'absurd.' What do you think the media is going to say when he says that?"

"What do you know about this guy? Can he be pressured?" caller one asked.

"That's the problem. I have thoroughly researched this kid, and here's what we know. This guy has done a lot to help my guys and my team. Plus, he's done it with little or no fanfare. He has kept stuff out of the papers that would result in major publicity headaches. I know enough that if we pressure him, it could blow up in our faces. Let me put it this way: Dave Smith of the *Dallas Morning News* is his buddy, and even Landry likes him. He seems to have the best interests of his players at heart. He is not like the agents who just negotiate contracts and take their cut. He's guiding them. Now he's being appointed municipal court judge. He was a chief prosecutor for Dallas. Before he moved to Dallas, he used to work for the agent of basketball player Walt Frazier at his sports agency in New York. I have a guy on my PR staff who knows him from the university they attended. He said he won't back off, especially if cornered. Coach Abe Lemons, who coached him and then hired him as the Assistant Sports Information Director while in law school, told my guy that if he could put his heart in the rest of his players, they would win the NCAA title. Hell, Landry just autographed a football for the sitting U.S. Attorney in Dallas, who happens to be a groomsman in this guy's wedding. You see what I'm talking about."

"Well, I guess we'll just have to wait and see ... continue to pressure the players till they fold up. Unless you have another suggestion," caller one replied.

The third voice interjected, "Tex, I'll be in Dallas tomorrow. Let's have lunch at the Mansion, and we'll discuss this in person."

"Fair enough," Tex said. "Call me in the morning."

"Fine, I'll talk with you both later."

The call ended. Tex turned to Wilson and said, "Just when everything was going the way we wanted it to, this little shit interferes. Do you know him well?"

Wilson responded carefully, "Yes, Tex. He helped Fitzy, Hegman, Cosbie, Smerek, and others with their personal matters. He is always polite and respectful to our staff. He knows the industry and how our contracts are structured regarding deferred compensation. He's never been a problem."

Tex met his lunch appointment at the Mansion. They discussed several issues pertaining to the new television contract and how this strike might affect things. Tex later described his entire meeting with me to him, nearly verbatim. The lunch guest asked whether he knew of anyone who might be able to influence this attorney without it feeling like pressure. Tex indicated that there was Doug Todd, his public relations guru, the employee he had mentioned on the phone the day before. "They aren't close, but maybe close enough to get something accomplished." Tex and his comrade agreed that Doug Todd should try to do his stuff before they pursued other avenues.

One week later, I received a telephone call from Don Wilson about a client's documentation that referred to his deferred compensation. We agreed that I would meet with Don at his office, as he had all of the in-depth files on the players that I had not yet retrieved. We were going over the terms of every deferred compensation agreement, and I heard the unmistakable voice of Doug Todd. "Look out, Don, that short guy's got a mean streak a mile wide. Trust me, I know. What do ya say, L. B.? Long time, no see."

Only someone from my era at my college would call me *L. B.* Coach Paul Hansen, my freshman basketball and varsity baseball coach, nicknamed me "Little Buddy" on the first day of unofficial basketball workouts. By the end of the afternoon, Coach Abe Lemons had shortened it to the initials *L. B.* With the exception of some of my professors, for the next seven years the school staff, faculty, and student body referred to me as L. B. A few old friends and classmates still do today.

"Hey, handsome," I replied.

Doug continued, "You guys almost done? L. B., lunch is on me if you can spare the time."

"Sure," I said. "I was going to eat in, but I could use the break. As soon as we wrap up here, I'll pop down to your office and pick you up."

"I'll be waitin'," he said.

Doug was a tall, slender Oklahoman who had also been the Assistant Sports Information Director at our university during the Division I power years of NCAA basketball under Coach A. E. "Abe" Lemons, the head basketball coach and athletic director. He was close to both Abe and Paul. We were also very close to Bud Koper (the All-American basketball player, NBA player, and sports information director), for whom Doug worked. I had become the Assistant SID under Bud Koper while I was in law school. Doug knew my characteristics and my temperament.

After our meeting, Don Wilson did something unexpected: he had the receptionist buzz Doug to meet me at the front desk so that I wouldn't be walking the halls of the Cowboys' organization. Funny thing, but that concern had never crossed my mind; I had the same policy implemented at our office from that day forward.

Doug and I decided we would take separate cars and meet at Caulfield's. We arrived at Caulfield's, and the owner showed us to a reserved table at which Don and I ate several times a week. We should have bought stock in the place. As we sat down, I was handed a note from the owner to call the office when I arrived. I excused myself and was escorted to the office, where I could have my conversation in privacy.

Lisa answered the phone and said, "Several of the players have called about their cars. Don told me to tell you that Noel said 'it's a heavy situation' that requires your immediate attention."

"Lisa," I said, "tell Noel I'm at a business meeting and tell him to call each player to get the details on their particular problem. Get all the information, including phone numbers. I'll be back at the office no later than 1:15."

I returned to the table and found that the owner had already ordered my favorite meal and was awaiting my return to serve Doug and me. Just as we were about to eat, Doug said, "Tex tells me you're representing guys from all around the league for this strike. How in the heck did that happen?"

I paused for a moment and very bluntly stated, "I knew this free lunch had a twist. Hitchcock is about to make his cameo...."

Doug laughed and said, "Really, L. B., why the hell are you getting involved in this crap—you crazy? Do you realize the type of people involved in this dispute? These people don't *play*."

I said, "Doug, I'm not going to have to get involved if people start doing the right thing by these players. That doesn't mean from just the owners' end. The union has big problems, too."

"I understand that; that's not my point. Why do you have to get involved in this stuff? Let the two sides iron it out themselves. What's a handful of players really capable of doing to this machine? You'll get stomped. Spence, you've got a bright future ahead of you. You've already made a mark in this business, even with the Cowboys. You've done a great job for your clients. Build on that and don't get involved with this strike. Let the labor talks handle it."

"Doug, really, thanks for your concern. I appreciate what you are saying. But I'm going to see how this all unfolds. Right now, all I'm really doing anyway is evaluating. That's all. If it were more, you probably would already know. Now, no more business talk. Let's enjoy our lunch. When is the last time you spoke with Abe?"

CHAPTER 17
Walk, Can't Ride

A view from Anthony Dickerson

I checked into my hotel room the night before our second game of the regular season and called a girl I'd met at Elan's to see if we could get together for dinner and drama Monday evening. This girl was fine.

She picked up the receiver, and I said, "Hey, beautiful. What you up to?"

"Anthony?" She was surprised to hear from me.

"It's me, baby. In the flesh.... Hey, what about us going out Monday after work? I'm off on Tuesday, so I won't be in a hurry to go home. What do you say? I'd love to see you."

"Let's see," she said. "We go out three days in a row, sleep together, and then I don't hear from you for weeks. You're pretty ballsy to think I would go out with you now just because you call me on the phone."

"Why? Didn't we have a great time together? Didn't you say that you couldn't wait to see me last time?"

"Yes ... but that was last time—three weeks ago." She wore a broad smile I could hear through the phone.

"Sweetie, you know I might be out of a job this week. Come on, I really want to see you," I begged boyishly.

"What about Thursday night instead?" she asked.

"You know I can't do that. Monday evening is the only safe time for me to plan something without feeling pressed about work. What do ya say? Please."

"All right. But only if you stay the night, and only if you don't hurry off in the morning."

"Great. Looking forward to it, baby. Hey, what do ya say you wear that black halter top? You look beautiful in that. Talk at you later."

I hung up the receiver and rested my head on my pillow, attempting to will a dream along the lines of what I was getting when I got back to town.

We arrived home from St. Louis fairly late. Although we were happy about the win we'd just delivered, we were all anxious for what tomorrow would bring. The air was filled with questions and unacceptable answers. I hitched a ride with Hegman (Mike Hegman was number 58, a graduate of Tennessee State. He played the strong-side linebacker; I played weak-side) and wandered over to the IHOP for a late breakfast. When I arrived home, the girls were asleep. As much as I wished that they would be awake, my exhausted body, my sore muscles were glad that the ladies were unavailable. I eased myself into bed and, surprisingly under the circumstances, fell asleep fairly quickly.

I woke up early the following morning in a pool of sweat. The air seemed thick and musty, and my body had changed from sore to painful. My muscles were unusually tender. I tried to squeeze my hand into a fist, but even my grip had become fatigued. It was weird. We had all pushed ourselves as hard as we could the other day, and it was clear that all of our bodies were going to pay for it. This must have been a rough morning for everyone on the roster. But I had my roommates: two foxes rattling around in the kitchen. By the time I pulled myself out of bed and peeked outside, the girls were gone.

They had prepared a gourmet breakfast for me (two eggs, toast, three strips of bacon) and had it covered with tinfoil on the stove. Wedged under a glass of orange juice was a note drenched in innuendo and sexual overtones. I liked how they looked after me—God knows how much I needed that attention back then. But despite the comfort of my living arrangements, I was completely unprepared for what was about to happen at work and the ramifications those events would create the next day and the days to follow.

Most of the time, just being around the girls was fun. They laughed just as much as they gossiped. It was an apartment filled with incessant chatter. Normally, that would have been just fine with me. But today was different. I was on edge when I woke, and I was on edge when I was chewing my eggs, which had been left just the right amount of runny. I was on edge, but certainly through no fault of the girls. Today the team would be informed of the date and time the labor walkout would begin. We had hoped that it wouldn't be for several weeks into the season, so that we could garner more checks to cope with the days of limited income.

But hoping doesn't get you too far. What the hell did we know? We were only the rank and file. We certainly weren't the union leaders.

Late Monday afternoon, I met my friend Kim for drinks before dinner at the Chateaubriand off McKinney Avenue and Fairmount in downtown Dallas. She was dressed in a silk blouse and knitted skirt that accentuated her finest attributes. A man could easily get lost in her slender, toned calves and thighs as she stood nearly five-foot-nine. Her beaming smile was filled with warmth and sincerity. I knew it was going to be a fabulous evening.

Pete Vouras, the proprietor, greeted us at the door. He was a suave and debonair man around forty who could charm the nose off your face. Naturally he had a place as elegant as he was—excellent food with quality service. It was the perfect place to ignore pressing thoughts of the impending strike, a place to spend some of those precious last dollars, the perfect place to get to know Kim a bit more.

We stayed until the place was virtually closing, just before Pete would dim the lights to brush off the stragglers. We were smiling and carefree as we approached her apartment. Once we entered, she quickly closed the door behind me and pulled me down to the couch. As she wrapped her extra-long legs around me, I could feel her heart pounding like a timpani drum. We stayed lip-locked for what seemed like hours. Eventually, we navigated ourselves to her bedroom. I was glad to be in "football playing shape" before meeting Kim. One certainly would have to be.

I did learn one important thing from spending the night with her: Kim's apartment would be the wrong place to be for a professional football player during the regular season. My survival instincts told me that the rigors of professional football and the addictive qualities of a beautiful woman like Kim wouldn't mesh too well. I was spent the moment practice wrapped; what stamina would I have left for her? On top of that, I realized money was going to be very tight. But, hell, I knew that I needed at least one last incredible time before the strike began. If I had to do it over, I still would have spent that money at the Chateaubriand.

As we expected, but sooner than we wanted, the union leadership designated that the rank and file would walk out after the second game of the regular season. That meant no money and two sets of regular-season bruises to remind us that we were all out of jobs.

That evening I drove over to Kim's place, simply—it turned out—to reinforce my realization of how important it would be to manage whatever funds I had left. I never made it to the door. I just drove off and headed back to my place, back to hang with the girls. We were all waiting to see what the owners would try to pull on us. Little did I know how imminent that would be.

I took a short stroll through a park early Tuesday morning, pondering what was lying ahead. I knew I would probably need a part-time job to carry me through the days that football was sidelined. The lone faded fifty dollar bill in my pocket told me that would have to happen relatively fast.

I woke that Tuesday blinded by the light shining through a curtainless window. The girls had already left for work. They had, once again, left breakfast for me. This didn't happen often, but they were being extra nice because of my tenuous job situation.

I felt weird that morning knowing I'd have to do part-time job interviews. For some reason, my morning rituals moved in slow motion. I sang my songs in the shower extra slowly, showered extra slowly, shaved extra slowly, and even seemed to dress extra slowly. It wasn't that I was in no hurry to get on with my day—I knew I needed the cash; it's just that I find time moves slower when you're dreading the present and near future.

I walked idly toward my parking space, mumbling to myself what I was going to say to these guys. *Where was my last job? Well, I play for the Cowboys....* I walked through my parking space, through the emptiness that the car I'd been loaned was supposed to fill. My first thought was that I must have parked it somewhere else. But I clearly remembered parking there. I started to panic a little. Forget the interviews. *What the hell am I going to tell the dealership? How the hell can I pay for this? Should I call the cops?*

I'll call the cops, report the incident, get people looking for it.... That won't work. I don't even know the make of the car, the year. I don't know its damn license plate number. What an incompetent fuckup.

With all these thoughts running through my head, I continued to search the complex parking lot area in hopes that I had, for some reason, parked in one of the girls' spots. Nope.

Left with no alternative, I realized I had to contact the dealership to inform them of what had happened. I called. The dealership already knew.

The general manager's assistant got on the line and said in, as far as I could tell, one breath, "Anthony, I am sorry but we had to retrieve the dealership's vehicle we loaned to you. We had no other choice. The arrangement for you to have a car was predicated on the fact that you would furnish the dealership four regular-season Dallas Cowboy game tickets for the NFL season. Since that season has been indefinitely interrupted, that arrangement is no longer in effect. When the season starts over, we will still welcome the arrangement. Oh, by the way, we did try to reach you but were unable to do so. Otherwise, we would have asked you to voluntarily return the vehicle.

Based upon our floor-plan requirements, we had no alternative. Once again, we are truly sorry for the inconvenience."

Trying to talk with this guy was like trying to talk with my old assistant principal at my high school. I couldn't get a word in, and even if I did, it didn't matter to him. He had an agenda, and I wasn't on it anymore.

I did, however, get the chance to squeeze in one very important question: "Excuse me, but can't I buy a car?"

"Well," he said, "I don't know. Technically, you are, at present, not receiving an income from the Dallas Cowboys. So, you would need to verify other means of employment to establish proof of income to meet your responsibilities under the car loan. Are you currently employed somewhere else?"

Stupid question.

He continued, "If not, there is little, if anything, I can do to assist you. I am truly sorry. However, if your situation changes, please do not hesitate to contact us. Good luck to you. I hope the strike ends soon."

With that, he hung up the phone.

I was totally floored by what had just happened. What could have instigated this conduct? They had to have known what they were going to do if they took such a drastic step as towing away their own car. Why not call me at work prior to the strike to inform me of their intentions? I called B. J. to confirm my speculation. Would the teams of the NFL have the audacity to get the dealerships to repo our loaner cars? You bet. Later on, I found out that similar events had happened throughout the league.

I called Noel to contact Spence to find out if there was anything he could do to help me. If there was anyone who would sincerely try to help, it was Noel and Spence. Noel indicated that I was not alone in this car fiasco. He promised me that he would get hold of Spence to see what could be done.

My alarm went off at 10:00 p.m. I struggled out of bed, dressed quickly, splashed some water on my face, and hurried over to my work assignment for the next eight hours—if you call it work.

I arrived at the office-building complex off Hillcrest Road near the LBJ Freeway at about 11:00 and met my supervisor for the evening. He gave me my work satchel and watering can. After speaking with him briefly, I proceeded to the lobby of the largest building to feed and water the plants and flowers that decorated the greeting area. That's right. You read it correctly. The starting weak-side linebacker of the professional football team that represented the metropolis of Dallas, Texas—no, America's Team—was supplementing his income by watering the decorative plants in the lobbies of office buildings. It was the quickest thing I could find, and I needed the money fast; like they say, beggars can't be choosers.

That early morning, just as I was completing my rounds quietly watering the plants lining the windows near the elevator banks, I noticed Captain Comeback, Roger Staubach, heading toward me. *Holy shit. What do I do?* The closer he got, the faster my heart raced. I hid behind the tallest plant as if I were adjusting leaves or branches or something. He ducked into the men's restroom about thirty feet away, but I was sure his eyes had met mine. Even though we had not played together, I had met him before, and I was fairly certain he would recognize me, if he hadn't already.

But suddenly I realized that he had given me a way out. Tears welled up in my eyes—I blinked, sending them down my face in two quick splashes. I gathered my stuff and quickly shot a beeline for the exit. I left the building without saying a word to my coworker. Later on, I would tell my coworker that I had become extremely sick to my stomach the moment I left—as badly as I was feeling, I did not have the luxury of time to locate him to inform him that I was leaving. In any case, my instincts were to get out of there as fast as I could.

Once I got home, I questioned whether Roger even knew it was me. I thought he did. And if that were true, he sure had saved me from an embarrassing moment. Either way, I vowed to myself that I would never be in that position again. Maybe it shouldn't have mattered to me—it *was* work. But it did matter; that was how low I felt.

It was abundantly clear to me that there was no "Strike Fund" to help me through this, and there was little or no chance that the union leadership was going to resolve the strike in a positive way for me or any other union members.

You know, at that point in my life, I wasn't prepared to face such huge, potentially life-changing encounters and decisions. But since the owners didn't care and the union leaders had no clue, that's just the way it was. Just think: the owners were so calculated that they didn't even care if our families had a car to drive; the union leadership, in its infinite wisdom in calling for the strike, had spent little if any time properly preparing its membership for what events or problems might arise during the interim before the strike. Something needed to be done, but it wasn't going to come from the union.

CHAPTER 18
Walk, Can't Ride ... Times Two

A view from Billy Joe DuPree

On the first official off day, I rose early in the morning to do my normal workout and two-mile run before leaving for the office of my construction company. When I arrived at the office, I showered and shaved, put on a suit and tied my tie, and began to prepare for the scheduled business meetings. I soon eased myself into my office chair, sipped on a cup of coffee, and began to read up on the scuttlebutt of the NFL strike.

I pulled the sports sections from the middle of the *Dallas Morning News* and the *Dallas Times Herald*, and then I remembered it was my "honey-do" responsibility to call home and make sure the boys would wake early to finish their homework from the night before. I dialed the phone, and my office administrator entered the office (after quietly rapping on the doorjamb) to inform me that both Larry Bethea and Rod Hill had called. My wife's phone line was busy. Well, I was just about to call Larry and Rod when I received a call from my wife, and she was angrier than a wet hen. She proceeded to lash out, literally damning the Cowboys' management, and though that wasn't new, her reason for being so enraged this morning was. When my wife went out to our driveway to drive our sons to school, she noticed her dealer car was not there. (Car dealers would give dealer cars for one year for four season tickets.)

Let me assure you that although my wife is not a mind reader, she is certainly intelligent. She immediately assumed that my employer had something to do with the disappearance of the dealer car. Let me tell you with absolute certainty, Mrs. DuPree was hot!

"Honey," she said, "I know those bastards had our loaner car taken. It's gone. Don't ask me to check the garage or check anywhere else. I park in the same spot every single day. I never change. And I am telling you that the *team* contacted the car dealership and had them tow your loaner car."

"Sweetheart," I replied, "I think you're right. It's just like I told the guys at our last team meeting before we went on strike: the owners will stoop to anything to create an advantage. They're trying to expose any vulnerability we might have. The car never crossed my mind."

"Personally," she added, "I don't care what they do. I do care what you and your teammates do. I am not comfortable with the way the union has planned this strike. Everything you and Rayfield say shows that the NFLPA is shooting from the hip. They don't have a damn clue what they're doing. None of what you had me read says anything about how they plan to achieve the necessary changes without losing the season or forcing the owners to make any significant changes." Marsha, having caught her breath, continued, "B. J., this type of 'leadership' has to stop if you guys are going to have any chance of getting things changed."

"Mom DuPree, tell me what you really think." I chuckled with admiration. My wife is one sharp lady, I'm here to tell you. "Marsha, I am going to meet with Rayfield for lunch today and go over what happened with the World Football League stuff that he and Csonka dabbled in. And I am gonna talk with House to see what he can shed light on. Maybe he can give me the true status of what's going on within the union leadership and its plan to streamline and legitimize its list of demands for more realistic concessions by the owners."

"That's good," said Marsha. "But ask Rayfield and anyone else who knows what the true concerns of the owners are and what the owners can't have happen—anything that would create a rallying point for the players. Come up with something like that, and you could create some unity within your union." She had said the same thing last night, when we still had a car. Now she was driving her point home. I could hear Marsha gathering her office materials, and I told her to use our third car, a Jeep Wrangler, a car owned by my construction company.

"Hopefully it will start," she said. "B.J., I am going to take the kids to school. After I do, I am going to have the Jeep checked out. I'll find a way home. Let me know where you are, in case I have trouble. You may have to pick the boys up from school, okay?"

"That's fine. But I would check the oil first before you drive very far. You don't want the engine to lock up. At this point, we will need that car operational, or at least in a fixable condition."

"B. J., don't you think I know that? Why do you think I am taking the car directly to the dealer after dropping the kids at school? I'll check the oil before leaving the house."

"Thank you, dear. I probably should have checked it already myself. My bad," I replied.

"Well, you couldn't have seen this part coming. I guess I'm a bit testy this morning. Wonder why."

"I perfectly understand. But that's why you're considered the better half. I'll check back with you later. Love ya."

"Love you too," she said. I could hear her open the creaking hood of the Jeep, and then she hung up.

I sat there thinking how fortunate I was to be married to such a wonderful companion, but soon I was interrupted once again by my office administrator. This time, she told me that Larry Bethea was holding on line two. "Thanks, Fran, I'll take it."

With that, I put my head back on the neck rest of my chair, slowly leaned over with my right arm toward the credenza, and lifted the receiver off its cradle. "Larry, what can I do for ya, big fella?" I asked.

"Well, for one thing, my car arrangement with the Ford dealer has been suspended, effective immediately. That leaves Gloria without wheels and me with a super headache. I just don't get it. What's the fucking deal? Don't the owners realize that they're just pissing us off even more than before?"

"Yup, I'm sure they do. But the teams don't have a conscience when it comes to the compensation or feelings of the players. You should know that by now."

"Isn't there anything we can do?" asked Larry. "You know, I'm not really confident in our union. Our advisors don't really advise. They talk to us like children—that is, when they talk to us at all. In fact, I can't remember the last time they spoke with us. All they tell us is to call our player rep if we have any questions or want an update. It's always a put-off, B. J. I'm sick of it."

"I agree. If you think it's bad being us, try being the player rep like House and you'll really feel up against it."

"I guess so," said Larry tonelessly.

Larry continued his rant of disapproval of the union leadership, and I wondered how unsettling the climate was getting around the labor dispute and the obvious choices that union leaders intended to make. It was becoming very clear that the choices being made for us were inadequate, inexcusably deficient. If we didn't do something soon, the results regarding proper labor terms, including but not limited to player compensation and health and retirement benefits, would be severely compromised. The time to deal with these matters was now. The question was how.

My life as I knew it had come to a major crossroads. Would I sit by and wait or would I seek other opinions and get to work on a solution? For the remainder of the day, I worked on tacks that might possibly resolve my problems. Frustration was setting in. I knew I would need help with this car situation.

When I arrived home that evening, my wife was ready with answers and questions of her own. Together we would come up with a plan for our family and others in the same dilemma. "B. J., this is our fight," she said. "The players, the wives, our families. These people are messing with our lives. This isn't just your fight. It's all of ours. Okay?"

"Okay," I replied. "I'm glad you feel this way. God knows how alone I'd feel if I didn't know you were behind me."

Marsha continued, "The players' wives have decided that we're going to pool our efforts. Set up a carpool for work and school."

"That sounds great. How many turned out?"

"A lot," she said. "Even wives of former players have offered to help. I'm confident that we can handle our end. So, what about the car?"

"Rayfield, Ron, and I are going over to each of our banks to get loans for cars that are being held for us at the used car lot—the one at the Ford dealership on Central Expressway. We're just going to get something simple to fit budgets. I'll call you from there when we're done so you can come by to execute the note."

"Okay, that works. Oh, the boys are shooting hoops out back. They're waiting for you by the garage. For a change, please remember they're your sons and don't block their shots tonight."

"Okay, Momma DuPree, I promise not to play Chamberlain."

Rayfield swung by to pick me up about 8:45 the next morning. We met Ron Springs and Larry Bethea at the Republic Bank at about 9:15. We were all anxious—that is, except for Rayfield. He was there to give support and keep things calm. He had been banking there for some fifteen years, and they treated him well. I, on the other hand, banked elsewhere. I didn't like the fact that the bank we were at was also one of our employer's banks. I would have to wait to go to Capital Bank on Mockingbird Lane, just five minutes away.

As we entered the confines of the bank, his loan officer's secretary greeted Rayfield warmly. After briefly visiting with Rayfield, the secretary excused herself and went across the lobby to the offices that were directly opposite the bank tellers and cashier. She briskly walked to one of the offices across the way and stepped inside. Once back in the lobby, the secretary signaled to Rayfield to bring the lot of us to a small conference room at the end of a narrow hallway.

We all sat down at a nine-foot rectangular conference table and waited for the loan officer. The secretary offered us refreshments, but only Rayfield asked for anything. With the voice of a preacher, he asked for a coffee. We waited for approximately thirty minutes before the banker entered the room. It felt like three hours. The meeting was short and bitter.

Larry started by telling this very young loan officer that he was at the bank to get a family car for his wife. At that point, the loan officer asked Larry to fill out an application form and to notify his secretary when he was finished. Though I did not know the banker, he appeared tense and methodical. He was certainly different from any banker that I had dealt with before. I realized later that the strange feeling I had wasn't due to the banker at all. It was just the vibe from the unfortunate situation this banker had been thrown into. Upon completing the application form and returning the document to the secretary, Larry returned to the conference room, confident that it wouldn't take very long. And was he right! A mere fifteen minutes went by before the loan officer re-appeared.

He sat down at the opposite end of the table, and with the secretary standing to his right by the door entryway, he said, "Mr. Bethea, on your application you state that your employer is the Dallas Cowboys Football Club, and you further specify that you are receiving an income in excess of one hundred thousand dollars. This application is based upon income as of this very day. However, Mr. Bethea, since you are currently on strike, your income as it pertains to professional football has been halted for an indeterminate period. The bank has no idea when—if—you will return to work. Technically speaking, unless you or your wife can show the bank an alternative adequate source of income that could verify your ability to pay the loan, the bank has no option other than to deny your application. I am truly sorry—we consider you a valued account holder. When the season starts again, please feel free to come to the bank so I can honor your request. Once again, I am truly sorry for not having the capability of assisting you today." Then, as he surveyed our forlorn faces, he rose from his chair to leave.

As he approached the door, Ron stood up and let out, "I know that this isn't your fault. But, Mr. Banker, this is pure bullshit." With that said, Ron left the bank. Even though he was upset, he knew that this young banker was merely a messenger boy.

Rayfield told the banker that he was willing to cosign on the loans until the season began. The banker repeated that it was out of his hands.

After that, no player I hung with ever banked there again. As we stood in the bank's parking lot and discussed what had just happened, Larry interrupted and suggested we contact Hegman, because he thought he had a guy who might be able to help. So we called Hegman, and sure enough—and much to my relief —he told us exactly what we should do and who to contact.

It was clear to all of us that what had just happened had been choreographed by the team. I don't know what they expected our reaction to be—despair? All it did was piss us off more and instill in us a greater resolve to succeed. It reminded me of something Vince Lombardi once told his players during a tough spot in their season on the way to a world championship. He said, "The harder you fight, the harder it is to surrender." No truer words were ever said.

CHAPTER 19
No Wheels

A view from Spencer Kopf

I returned to the office and was greeted by a stack of phone messages from players up in arms about their cars. At first, I didn't understand the problem they were having: "Where's my car, Spence? My car's been stolen, Spence." But, after I returned the call from Anthony Dickerson, it all became quite clear. Each year, players of major sports teams would make arrangements with certain car dealerships, wherein players would provide a package of prime season tickets (usually four) in exchange for the use of a vehicle for twelve months. Since the season was halted after the first two games, the dealers were retrieving their cars from the players until the season started again. Few players had planned for that contingency, so they found themselves without the use of a car. For some, it meant that they were without a family car, which created havoc within the family and neighborhood circles. For others, it meant they were walking.

The dealers had not only scuttled school carpools but grocery trips as well.

I previously had asked Noel to gather a complete list of players who were affected by this vehicular paralysis. It took Noel approximately an hour to gather the information and schedule the times for each player to come in. I put a call in to Larry Lange, a close friend and a highly respected car dealer in north Texas. I asked if I could meet him after work to discuss this problem and see how it could be resolved. Larry already was providing some cars to players; but, unlike the other dealers, he was not reneging on his arrangements. He knew the strike was out of the players' control and knew they needed all the support they could get. I asked Noel to tell Anthony to stay by the phone that night—I had a way to get him some wheels, at least temporarily.

The drive to McKinney seemed longer than usual that evening. Traffic was extremely heavy, and it started to rain. I had frequently met with "Double"—a moniker Larry had received because of the two Ls of his name. He is a close friend and confidant. There are few men like him. Larry is compassionate yet tough, trustworthy, reliable, and loyal. I knew he was probably the only guy who had the temerity to stand by these players simply because it was the right thing to do. The rain was coming down heavily—nature's foreshadowing of the months to come.

Two years earlier, one of my clients had a ticket arrangement with Larry. The player, for insurance purposes, was not permitted to lend the car to any other person: he and his spouse were the only people allowed to drive the car. Unfortunately, this client loaned the car to another player, who subsequently trashed it. Larry called my office to inform me of the situation. I confirmed the problem with the client and made an appointment to meet with Larry at his dealership in McKinney off Central Expressway.

The significance of that first meeting with Larry was that I committed to him that if the client did not have the balance of the damages paid off within two weeks' time, I would pay the balance myself. This, unfortunately for me, is exactly what happened. I eventually was reimbursed, but at the time, it was more important to me to value such a relationship and honor the trust he had put in my client. That, apparently, was all Larry Lange needed to know. Regardless of the problem, it pays to always be straight, especially with Double.

Anyhow, here I was, trying to assist players who were now not only being traumatized by management, but by no-tickets-no-car deals. We later learned that these same dealerships had similar arrangements with the management and coaches. The teams had contacted the dealers and instructed them to call in the cars. The car dealers capitulated. Of course, the management and coaches' cars remained as they were: they lay parked and pampered in their garages.

I arrived at the dealership at approximately 5:30 p.m. I walked in the main entrance, traveled down a narrow hallway to the left, and entered Larry's office. As I entered, Larry rose to his feet. Larry Wayne Lange was a former college athlete from the University of Northern Iowa; he stood right at six feet tall. He was well-built, had strong handsome features, was slightly balding on the top of his head, and had a smile and voice that captivated. He had married his college sweetheart, and they had four children. Mary was Larry's rock. She was an attractive, intelligent woman whose devotion to her family and friends was without equal. And Larry could sell an ice cube to an Eskimo during a blizzard.

He bounded around his desk, having paused the conversation he was having with two of his salesmen, and bellowed, "Fellas, meet my little buddy, Spencer Kopf—the workingman's friend and the people's choice. What took so long? Traffic bad?" With the same breath in his lungs, he continued, "Phil, take over from here. Please have the final numbers available for me for tomorrow morning's sales meeting. Spence and I are going to head over to the Inn for a few shooters. You can join us when you're through, if you like." At that, Larry whisked me out the door toward our cars. We were over at the bar within two minutes. I ordered a Coors and Larry a Grey Goose.

"What do you think about it, Double?" I blurted out almost immediately after our order was taken.

Larry quickly and firmly responded, "It's hard to believe that these guys, these owners, think that pulling these stunts against the players is going to weaken their desire to fight. I'll tell you this: it would do the opposite to me. It would piss me off. In fact, it does piss me off, because some of the players, as you know, are friends of mine." He paused for a second to chew his gum and draw the attention of our waitress with a raised hand. He asked, "You got any pretzels or peanuts, darlin'?"

"Be right there, Larry," she replied.

I interjected, "Double, Anthony Dickerson ..." (who gave me permission to divulge his financial info to verify the depth of his dilemma) "makes around twenty-eight thousand base, with very little chance of achieving his incentive bonuses. Without that car deal and without team paychecks coming in, he is in deep dogshit. This kid waters plants at commercial buildings as a side job to bring in some cash. It's sick how these teams treat these guys."

"Spence, the owners operate under the 'Golden Rule' of business: the people with the gold make the rules. This has nothing to do with anything but control. Plain and simple. Guys who do that lose sight of what is important in running a business. Believe me, the owners one day will regret not treating their employees right. If your employees don't feel like they are being treated fairly, it will always come back to bite you in the ass. People work better when they enjoy their work and the people they work for. Trust me, I know." In all the years that I have been around Larry, I have not met a single member of his staff who didn't enjoy working for him.

After discussing the players with Larry, we worked out a scenario whereby the players could earn the use of the vehicles by making personal appearances at his dealership at various times until the season restarted. Obviously, those appearances were just a way to accommodate the players' needs while effectively justifying his favor. In the long run, it was a win-win for everyone, and the players never forgot Larry's friendship and aid. Naturally, other dealership owners presently followed suit once they saw how successfully Larry had utilized the players' celebrity.

The first player to meet with Larry was Anthony Dickerson. Anthony had played his college ball at SMU and was familiar with Larry. They visited for quite some time and arranged for Anthony to make appearances that would be advertised by the dealership. The same arrangement was made with each of the other players in need of a vehicle. It was the responsibility of each player to meet with Mr. Lange in person to arrange the dates and times of their appearances. Noel was responsible to monitor the appearances. If they failed to honor their commitment, they would forfeit the privilege to use the vehicle. Throughout the entire strike, the players honored their commitments to Larry. And Larry, of course, honored his.

Later, I was informed that Larry even assisted some of the guys with cash advances on future appearances until the strike ended so that they could weather the storm of no income. Larry was pleased with the outcome and was, specifically, very reassuring during this tumultuous time. He would always remind me of the principles that our college coaches had instilled in us. I once shared the old Lombardi chestnut with Double: "The harder you fight, the harder it is to surrender." He had said, "I know that one, Spence. How true that statement is in sports and in life." During the stresses of the strike, Larry would continue to play a major role in our persevering. Since then, he has been a great influence in my life. He will not let a friend endure unjust hardship alone. He is treasured by me and by my two sons. I know few men his equal.

CHAPTER 20
Media Outlook

A view from Scott Murray

I arrived in Texas in 1981 to work at the NBC affiliate in the Dallas-Fort Worth metroplex as sports director/anchor. In taking my new position, it was my desire to do something that would set us apart from the other local affiliates as a way of establishing instant credibility from the viewers. I convinced the station management that an extended Sunday night sports wrap-up show would be a sure home run. I had anchored such a show with my previous employer, NBC in Washington DC, so I thought it would be a sure hit in a market that played home to America's Team. Despite some initial rejection, within days, Scott Murray's Sports Extra had become the first expanded Sunday night sports show in the Southwest. Within a year, we were number one in the ratings. It was a fun time, being a part of such a pioneering concept. Providing an entertaining, yet accurate and informative, product on the world of sports was our top priority. Share as much information as possible, and let the viewer form his own opinion on what was going on.

As someone who initially had planned to pursue a career in pediatrics, I was always anxious to spend spare time working with children's charitable and nonprofit organizations. Such involvement allowed me to spend much of my free time in the community, working with worthy organizations that were making a difference.

As the summer passed, I found myself booked as a guest speaker at many local events, specifically educational and religious organizations, municipal sport associations, and corporate awards banquets. It was early November in 1981 when I spoke at a Men's Club luncheon at the Shearith Israel Synagogue of Dallas. One of those in the audience happened to be a young, brash attorney named Spencer Kopf.

I had actually first met Spencer when I interviewed him regarding one of his clients, Don Smerek. The former Dallas Cowboy player had been involved in a shooting the previous month. As I recall, it had been a short, concise, tight question-and-answer session. Spence didn't lack confidence. He was always tight-lipped unless he really wanted to get something circulated in the media. The information I received was general in nature; Spence was firm in his resolve to protect the best interest and well-being of his client. I respected his position then, as I have done with all individuals I interviewed throughout my career.

As I began to learn that morning and throughout the years that followed, I could count on the accuracy and integrity of what I was told by Spence regardless of the subject matter discussed. He was not shy with his opinion or the facts in support of that opinion. He rarely rendered an opinion without having some significant information in support of his stance, whether popular or unpopular. But the key was the trust that he established with me. I came to know I could count on him for the correct information, even though it might not have made total sense or seemed to at the time.

As a point of interest, years later, Spence provided legal representation to assist several Texas Christian University (TCU) football players who were released from the team by Head Football Coach Jim Wacker for violating NCAA rules. The public and media perception were based on skimpy information and, therefore, a bit exaggerated and speculative. When I approached Spence for his clients' side, he requested I be patient as he did not want to jeopardize the best interests of his clients or breach attorney-client privilege. He further stated that providing any information based upon what was presently known would be premature. He assured me an accurate and substantiated story when his negotiations with the TCU attorney and the NCAA investigators were completed. In the meantime, we waited patiently, while providing updates until that time. In the end, channel 5 broke the story that all of the player scholarships to finish school academically had been reinstated, and the balance of the story was presented based on the facts and interviews that were now made available. Once again, as it always is, the truth was worth the wait—although I recall Spence being blasted by the press for being unwilling to divulge any information until he deemed it appropriate for his clients.

When the year 1982 arrived, it was filled with anxious anticipation because of the potential walkout (strike) of the members of the National Football League Players Association. The Collective Bargaining Agreement would end on July 15, 1982.

Covering that story would be a difficult chore at best because of the closed-mouth tactics being employed by the union leadership, both toward the press and, as I would learn later, oddly and quite significantly, toward and with its own membership. Additionally, the union leadership was trying to get the membership to approve a resolution that would have each union member have its individual employment contracts with their individual team negotiated by a representative of the union leadership. If that were passed, no player would be permitted to have his own individual agent or lawyer act on his behalf. The union leadership found that ploy to gain virtual total control of each union member's affairs to be a monumental mistake with their constituents. As it turned out, it was a huge blunder on the part of the union leadership, appearing to create an aura of instant and deep distrust within its membership. In the eyes of the members, the union leadership appeared to have been outmaneuvered by the owners' representative at every single turn. Thus, the longer the strike continued, the more incompetent and unsure the union leadership appeared.

On the other hand, the owners were taking a "matter-of-fact" position regarding the demands of the leadership of the players' union. They found the demands made by the NFLPA to be absurd and without justification or merit. With the union lacking the capability of establishing any factual position of leverage that would jeopardize the financial bottom line of the owners, the owners would have little or no reason to succumb to union demands.

The players were clearly disgusted with the position the owners were taking regarding the low salaries, inadequate retirement, lack of medical or disability benefits, and last but not least, no legitimate free agency format for players to shop their wares.

The situation regarding medical treatment provided to each player was also a major concern to the union and each of its members. In fact, the *Dallas Morning News* (July 11, 1982) had an article by Mark Blaudschun and Gary Myers regarding the Catch-22 that the team doctors were in regarding the medical services provided to each injured player. The doctors were caught between their employers (the team) and the athletes they treated. One particular story worth mentioning was the fact that an NFL team "knew that their field goal kicker, Rafael Septien, had played much of the previous season with a hernia, but failed to tell him."

Additionally, although the union rank and file had voted affirmatively to strike in an effort to seek equitable changes, the union members were quickly becoming disenchanted with the union leadership. This lack of confidence grew daily until it started to turn to the more serious mode that the membership no longer trusted its leadership, regardless of what they said or claimed to have done.

Oddly, everyone—the fans, the owners, and the union leadership—had little regard for the commencement of the United States Football League's upcoming season. However, some fans did render opinions to the news station that they were concerned that some of the more prominent players from their favorite team might jump to the USFL, thereby weakening their team among the other NFL teams.

As the collective bargaining agreement discussions commenced, the owners had chosen Jack Donlan to be their representative at the negotiation table. He had gained some notoriety by negotiating certain labor disputes for National Airlines. When National Airlines merged with Pan American, he was hired as the Executive Director of the NFL Management Council in 1980. Donlan was often known to flex his short Irish temper. That did anything but ingratiate him to his opponents. His argumentative and arrogant demeanor as a negotiator showed little respect for the union's Executive Director,

Ed Garvey. The NFLPA had chosen Ed Garvey because he had some labor law experience, following graduation from law school in 1969.

The mediator would be Sam Kagel. Kagel had a long history of dealing in labor relations; however, his selection to act as the arbitrator in this labor dispute was considered by many experts as questionable due to his condescending tone and abrasive manner. Since there was already a volatile person representing each side of the debate, the addition of Kagel was questioned by many. As it turned out, the experts' speculation concerning Kagel's participation eventually proved to be right on target, as he would return to his home on November 6, 1982, with the strike still in progress. Ironically, when the final terms and conditions of the 1982 collective bargaining agreement were reached, Sam Kagel was nowhere to be found.

In preparation for the upcoming clash with the owners, the NFLPA sought to raise the membership dues in 1981. Following a lengthy debate, the dues were increased from $670.00 to $850.00. The union leadership was seeking an increase to $1,122.00, but failed. This move of increasing dues was seen as a calculated act to build a war chest in the event a strike became necessary.

Another significant reason that a strike appeared to be imminent was the finalizing of new television contracts with the three major national television networks (ABC, CBS, and NBC), negotiated in great part by Dallas Cowboys' President and General Manager Tex Schramm. Although the terms of those contracts were, at the time, not made available to the media, the general remuneration information was.

In the final year of the previous television package, the funds divided among the twenty-eight teams allowed for each team to receive approximately $5.8 million dollars per year.[6] In 1982, the

6   Berry, Gould, and Staudohar, *Labor Relations in Professional Sports*, p. 128.

1982–87 economic package provided approximately $14.2 million dollars for each team. Understandably, the players felt they deserved a fair share of those funds.

Simply as a point of reference, in the 1982 winter meetings, the league had arranged for a $150-million-dollar line of credit with banks to help address the needs of the owners through the strike. This had become necessary because there had been no adequate "work stoppage" insurance available in the wake of the Major League Baseball strike.[7]

As each day of the strike passed, it was becoming apparent that the plan of the leadership group lacked foresight and substance, resulting in the disintegration of their support group. In fact, it was happening so fast that the handpicked selected team representatives were beginning to abandon the union leadership hours before the strike would be settled. Meanwhile, the media was being told the players were getting ready to return to work any day, even though they likely wouldn't have a contract.

After realizing that their demands for 55 percent of the gross was a pipe dream, the union leadership sought to seek a general wage scale increase across the board, with specific adjustments based on the years of playing time in the league by each player.

As the members of the media would later find out, the union leadership was not directly keeping the rank and file informed of what was transpiring or what their plan might be as far as leverage against the owners. All communication was restricted to the player representatives only from each individual team, and that communication was always infrequent and insufficient.

The owners were aware of the financial conditions of most of the players in the league, so they felt confident they could wait them out

7 Berry, Gould, and Staudohar, *Labor Relations in Professional Sports*, p. 141.

until the union imploded, leaving the players with no option other than to walk across the picket line. It was no secret that the majority of the players were financially strapped, if not broke.

Another indication that the union was ill prepared was the timing of the union's decision to strike. The union struck after the second game of the regular season. Had it waited until after the third game, each player would have automatically vested another full year credited to their pension, in addition to having received another paycheck to help ease the pain of the strike.

Most of the fans were frustrated at the players. They wanted football to return. And since compensation packages were not disclosed to the public, the players appeared selfish and greedy. Additionally, the players failed to cooperate with each other, thinking that much of the information was private. But when they began to find out such was not the case, tempers began to be tested—especially when they found out that an inferior player on one team might be making much more than a star player on another team.

The issues regarding the battle lines of the 1982 strike became quite clear and simple. As we would come to find out, both the players and the public had been deliberately misinformed by both sides of the negotiations. Strange but true. Additionally, both sides continued to withhold pertinent information from the media, the public, and the arbitrator, while providing information that never proved to be totally correct.

There is no question the players were uninformed and unprepared to enter into a strike, for both economic and emotional reasons. In hindsight, it appears the players were waging a battle on two fronts: not only were they battling the owners for better wages and conditions, but maybe more importantly, their own union leadership—a union leadership drenched in arrogance, manipulation, and distrust, attempting to achieve its own unachievable goals—all of this in hopes of posturing themselves into a position that would eventually benefit the personal desires, needs, and goals of a select greedy few.

While the media was left to try and figure out who was legit and who was talking trash, the hour of reckoning was fast approaching. The union leadership was out of steam. Player reps were leaving New York the night before the strike would end, after being informed that a scheduled meeting involving all of the player representatives had been called off. Most thought they'd be returning to work under the old terms without a new agreement. All had been for naught. The owners had apparently won because the union leadership had no leverage to force their hand. That was consistent with most of the information we were receiving from the owners' representatives. Or so it seemed.

In recalling the mood of the moment the day before the parties settled their differences, the majority of news sources were reporting that the owners were steadfast and unwilling to ease off their position, while the union leadership's support was buckling around them.

For close to sixty days, a solution to the strike and all of the adversity that accompanied it seemed futile. And now, close to three decades later, what was accomplished and how it was achieved still remains astonishing. To think that a lone group of men, against almost insurmountable odds, quietly committed, incredibly focused with unmatched resolve, put an end to close to half a season of "no football," is a testament of trust, confidence, and respect for one another like few others.[8]

---

8 Data on Garvey, Donlan, Kagel, Martha, union dues, and television contracts taken from Berry, Gould, and Staudohar, *Labor Relations in Professional Sports*, pp. 126–129, 137, 140–41.

CHAPTER 21
The Pressure Mounts

A view from Spencer Kopf

I was married October 16, 1982, left October 17 for the honeymoon, and returned to Dallas on October 20. It was not enough time to fully recharge my batteries, but it was enough time to contract Montezuma's revenge. I had never felt so sick in my life. I barely survived the flight home or the three days that I lived in the bathroom. (*Never* eat a salad in Puerto Vallarta unless *you* have washed the lettuce in purified water.) When I returned to work, you would have thought that Chicken Little's prediction had come true. Apparently, the sky was falling.... The players on the lower end of the pay scale and those who were overextended because they had not budgeted properly were calling the office every day for some sort of assistance.

Most of the players were represented by other agents, typically the kind who either did not—or could not—provide adequate legal assistance beyond contract negotiations. Those players felt abandoned and helpless. Representatives who did attempt to provide assistance in dealing with the union were met with the union's stone wall of misleading information and the patented excuse that "all information for the players can be obtained by each player by contacting their team representative with the NFLPA." Remember, Garvey wanted to replace the individual player representatives with union representatives. Absurd but true.

I asked Garvey directly, "How do you overcome the obvious conflict of interest in dealing with each player contract?" His response was so generic and parochial, it doesn't warrant the cost of the ink to put it to print; he—dodging the question—said simply that the union could be trusted. "All players will be treated equally." Well, thank goodness for that. You'll remember that I had also asked Garvey how he would avoid a conflict of interest by representing *all three* tight ends on the Dallas Cowboys, each believing he should start. "Mr. Garvey, how do you determine the pay schedule of that position when you represent all three men?" He said nothing and walked away. Garvey's attempted leadership of the NFLPA was an insult to the intelligence of each member of the union.

As the days of the strike mounted, any remaining confidence in the union leadership dramatically vanished. It was one thing to deal with no cars—soon they would be out of money. But the real thorn was that it was increasingly apparent that the union membership was becoming more disturbed and exasperated with the arbitrator, Sam Kagel.

Late in the afternoon of the fifty-third day of the strike, B. J. and Fred Dean crossed paths with Larry Bethea in Expressway Tower. After the introductions, Larry said to B. J. and Fred, "Did you see what Springs told the *News* the other day? Listen to this...." He then read from the newspaper: "'Do you believe this guy Kagel?'" said Ron Springs (fullback for the Dallas Cowboys). "He recessed the labor talks October 24. The talks stopped on the 47th day and here it is the 53rd day and the arbitrator is some three thousand miles away. Doesn't he seem concerned?'"

"Did you read the last bit?" B. J. added. It referred to Kagel. "He said, 'I think both sides should re-examine and reassess their positions.' Is he kidding?"

"B. J., do you think I can meet with Spencer and join your group of rebels?" Larry Bethea asked.

"I don't know. I'll be meeting with him tomorrow. He's really protective of his clients and expects cooperation. Do you think you can control your 'slightly opinionated' conduct? Spence needs compliance, not defiance, right about now."

"Well, under the circumstances," said Larry, "I probably could use a pit bull. I've got bills to pay. I'm choking on them. So is—"

"—Me!" B. J. interrupted. "I'm choking, too, Larry. I'll call him to set up a time. See if you can check with some of the other guys and let me know what they want to do. Larry, we're Spartans, remember."

"B. J.?"

"Yeah?"

"You think that little guy can do it?"

Fred Dean interjected, "As long as we stand behind him.... I'll tell you this: he won't back off from anyone, I'm not kidding. Listen, Larry. Me, Groove, and our friend Rasha were playing hoops at Texas Southern against Spence and two other guys that we picked up at the court. That little shit was kicking our asses all over the gym. I mean one serious ass-kicking. He drove to the bucket, bounced the ball between Rasha's legs, picked it up on the other side, faked a hook shot, which faked Noel off his feet, and Spence put an underhand layup in the bucket under Groove's arm. Really pissed us off. He's not laughing, no facial expression, nothing. He just went back to playing. Next time he drove to the hoop, Groove and I sandwiched him to the floor. The little shit still made the bucket. He was on the ground flopping like a fish out of water … one crushed by over 600 pounds. Then he got up and still said nothing. Nothing.… Later, he's way ahead, and someone from his team throws a dirty elbow. Larry, no shit, I thought Spence was gonna tear his head off. The guy was six-three, and he backed off of Spence! I kid you not. We were going to let it ride, but Spence wouldn't tolerate it. I've seen him on court and in court, in meetings, and on the phone with Bobby Beathard, General Manager of the Washington Redskins. The only person I have seen him back off of is his mom, and that's no lie. She's five feet nothing, and he backs off. Must be where he gets it. Ask Groove."

"He's right, Larry. He can't be bought, and the owners know it. Either way, what do we have to lose? We aren't getting anywhere with the union pushing for us, are we?" B. J. asked.

"No, guess not. Can I call you in the morning to meet?" Larry asked.

"Talk to you tomorrow," said B. J.

As Larry left, B. J. turned to Fred and said, "Fred, Spence can really shoot the rock?"

"Dupe, that ain't the half of it. Spence took our All-American to school at TSU. I mean, brother, it was ugly. Spence set the rules in a game of HORSE. No shot inside an arc starting at the top of the key, and Spence got to shoot first because he was playin' on the TSU floor. Dupe, brother, I mean it was ugly. That little shit didn't miss, I mean period. He set that brother up—skunked him two straight games. And that kid's never been the same. All that cockiness gone. Just like that. Worse, Groove knew it was gonna happen, and *he* took all the guy's bread. I'm telling you, if he is playing you in a game of checkers, pool, bowling, whatever, he will try to take your heart. He'll play fair, but I mean it: no mercy. Ha! When we were done playing him at TSU, we never wanted to play him again."

"Well, Fred, he must really like me, because he wants my ass on the golf course again real soon. I've got to get home to the wife. Check with you tomorrow," said B. J. as he moved to leave.

"Oh, man, you kiddin' me? You took the Chief down at golf, B. J.? Oh, man, I gotta tell Groove. We're gonna be all over him," said Fred.

"Hey, wait a minute—just forget I told you. We want him concentrating on helping us, right? Tell Noel to set a meeting for Bethea, okay?"

"I'll set it up with Noel, but there's no way I'm not gonna bring up the golf. No way."

"Fred ...," B. J. pleaded.

"Nope, this is too sweet. Later, Dupe," Fred laughed.

"Later," B. J. said as he turned, laughing his deep laugh.

Billy Joe: How'd we do it?

Tony: Yeah—what was the plan?

Joe: Well, they found a weakness. The owners and union had dug a hole for themselves; Spence just found the shovel and decided to finish the job.

Tony: Yeah. How?

CHAPTER 22
The Strategy

A view from Spencer Kopf

The players felt as if time were passing to the pace of a New Orleans funeral procession; the moment of confrontation, however, was approaching quickly. Our cadre conceptualized the date, time, and process of "The Plan" and its implementation. Once it was initiated, the players in our group needed to be steadfast. If they were as unified as they were in the week of preparation before a playoff game, they would succeed. I told Noel that the day we went forward with The Plan, I would examine the players to determine if that resolve was present. If I didn't believe it was as strong and as adamant as it needed to be, we would not go forward.

The strategy was simple. Our group of disenchanted members of the union would notify their leadership representatives, through me, that a legal pleading had been prepared for filing within the continental United States. This pleading would declare that the union leadership needed to show cause as to why they should not be restrained from representing their constituents. The pleading would be based upon verified statements that claimed the union's conduct was detrimental to the basic interests of each and every union member, regardless of roster or financial status. We would give the union a window of three hours and forty-five minutes to respond before we filed the papers. That timing was crucial. This short window would negate the expansive power of the owners—they would be unable to prevent a thing.

We would effect an immediate halt of the labor talks process. This would be an additional delay, which technically would be imposed by the court for a period not to exceed fourteen days. No matter how long it would turn out to be, the delay would be outside the effective control of either the owners or the union. That meant, for a specific period of time, those two groups would be powerless. The owners would know that without control of the strike, the season would be in jeopardy ... as would, consequently, the newly negotiated, 2.5 billion dollar television contracts. The union leaders would know that if others became aware that some of their own members pursued this legal process against them, the leaders' ability to operate as directors would be compromised at best and, in all probability, dissolved.

The only solution to the potential demise of the football season would be for both the owners and the union to immediately capitulate. If they did before The Plan was effectuated, both could save face without anyone besides the participants having any knowledge of what had transpired. Of course, capitulation meant severing egos and remunerating the players in a manner commensurate with their demands.

CHAPTER 23
Big Brother Intervenes

A view from Spencer Kopf

The strike was entering week six, and nerves were wearing thin. Family pressures: heavier. The union's demands, as asserted by the arbitrator: falling on the owners' deaf ears.

Other Expressway Tower tenants looked at our office with disdain. Outsiders with knowledge of my involvement with certain union members took me for an instigator and opportunist. But who could blame the bystanders for such tainted, prejudicial views? They were spoon-fed information by demagogues and gossip artists—drastically inaccurate information. (The minimum of facts with a side of fatuous fabrication.) The tension had billowed from trough to crest: the time to proceed with The Plan was near.

Reporters called nearly every hour and came to sniff the office air practically every day, unfazed by our no-comment-at-this-time-thank-yous. Then one day, late in the afternoon, a call came into the office that was more than annoying. Lisa answered the phone as she always did ("Law Office …"), and a deep male voice bayed, "Tell that short fucking Jew lawyer to back the fuck off or we'll fuck him up. You tell him!" Lisa immediately went down the hall to Noel and nervously reported the call. Noel told her that he would answer the phones the rest of the day. "Lisa, try not to worry about it."

Noel told me what he'd said: "Lisa, really, don't worry about it. If somebody wanted to do something, they'd do it without warning us first. They just want the Chief to back off, that's all. Hey, if they did do something to him, it would just really piss the players off. They know that, trust me. Really, it will be all right. Listen, girl, I'll call Fred. He'll stay with Spence until this deal is over with. If anybody even got this close to him, Fred would tear them apart. I'll tell you what, I'll call Fred right now. Just sit right here.…"

Noel called Fred, who was in Houston visiting some former teammates and checking on his house. Noel relayed the following conversation:

"Fred, check it out. Someone just called the office and threatened to hurt the Chief—shook Lisa up pretty good."

Fred yelled, "What?! Did she recognize the voice?"

"No. But she's real upset. When are you coming back to Dallas?"

"Now. I'll be there in about seven hours. You hang with Spence until I get there. You think I should bring Rasha with me? He'd be happy to help. He really likes Spence, and he's one bad brother, right?"

"He is, but I don't think we should do that. Rasha's not a player, and he doesn't work here. I mean, if he were here, he'd draw attention to the fact that something might be wrong. Anyway, the two of us are plenty. Plus, I doubt the city police would like someone who is threatening their city judge, I'll tell you that."

Fred then asked, "Man. What's going on, Groove?"

Noel responded sincerely, with certainty, "Fear, man. Whoever it is, they're afraid whatever the Chief is up to is gonna fuck with their world. Fred, look, if they were sure of themselves, they wouldn't resort to this."

"Probably not."

"Plus, what is it that the Chief has that they don't?"

"What?"

"Respect. Whoever it is knows that the Chief has more respect than the owners. Right now, who would fuck with what he is doing? As good as Spence has been with his players, other players, and other people he has helped. Remember his wedding? Wasn't it a who's who? If anything happened to him, those big people would turn over every rock and fuck those people up."

Fred nodded and said, "Right, but there are some crazy motherfuckers out there. So, I'm still coming up. Hey, I'm calling Clarence—" (Clarence Harmon, starting fullback for the Washington Redskins) "—about this shit. I'm gonna get his ass up here. Man, these people have to know that this stuff has to stop."

Noel responded, "Fred, remember this shit isn't about football. It's about what we discussed at the other night's meeting."

"Control?"

"Right, control. Both sides want a part of it and will do whatever it takes to get it. Remember what the Chief and Dupe said. If we create an equal playing field where there is less control and more fair play, the strike has to end. The owners and the union won't be able to fade the heat if the season ends."

Fred said abruptly, "Noel, do me a favor."

"What, big fella?"

"Get me two orders of Carolina Baby Back Ribs over at Tony Roma's before they close. I'll be starving when I get back in town. I'll make you tight when I see you."

Noel laughed, "You haven't paid me back since you were a freshman at TSU, but you will tonight."

"Later," Fred concluded.

"Drive safe," said Noel.

The next morning, Fred and I went to the office a little later than usual; my tires had been slashed at the office parking lot the previous afternoon. We had to deal with that when Fred arrived. Noel met us in the lobby, and we headed down the hallway to my office. Lisa went back to the main entrance and posted a sign on the door. The sign instructed unscheduled visitors to make an appointment by telephone or check with security downstairs to seek entry. Lisa shut the door and slammed the dead bolt home.

Noel approached her. "Lisa, we don't need to do that. What happens if the press came by? They would blow this thing way up. No one's doing nothing. There are going to be so many of us big guys here over the next several days, no one would dare. We'll be with the Chief everywhere till this is over. I'll tell you what, I'll man the front desk, and you take my office for the next several days."

"Are you kidding me?" asked Lisa incredulously. "You're going to be the greeter for this law office? That's rich. Guess again. Just close the entry door to the back area and have someone sit at the paralegal desk near that entrance. That way no one will try to get back there without one of you guys knowing. Oh, yeah, I ordered lunch in for everyone—took it out of the office petty cash."

"What did you order?" Noel asked, slightly dazed by Lisa's regenerated pep.

"What's the difference? You guys will eat whatever's placed in front of you anyway," she quipped, adding a brisk giggle.

"It's true," Noel admitted.

As lunchtime approached, a telephone call came in from someone who identified himself as my "big brother." When Lisa attempted to notify me of the call, I was in a conference with Fred, Noel, B. J., Norm, and Anthony. Lisa came back to my office and politely interrupted, "Excuse me, but your big brother is on line two. What should I tell him? Do you want me to take a message?"

What? I said to myself. I hadn't spoken to my older brother in about four years. So, I asked, "Who did you say was holding?"

"He said he was your big brother," she replied.

Well, that floored me. At that time, my older brother and I were not exactly close. Noel was well aware of that and asked me, "Do you want us to step outside?" I pondered his question—I thought there was a possibility that something had gone wrong back home in New York. But if that were true, I would have received a call from several other people first. "No, I'll take the call, find out what's on his mind, excuse myself, and agree to call him later. Just keep your seats."

I picked up the phone. "Hello," I said.

"Hello, Brother Kopf. It's sure been a long time since the leadership conference. I see you've been quite busy. The senator would be proud." Not my older brother. It was, however, someone I deeply respected and admired.

I responded, slightly forcing self-assurance, "Thank you, sir. To what do I owe the honor of this call?" As I held the receiver tilted away from my ear so all those present could hear, I wrote down the caller's name and handed it to B. J. He read it and passed it to the others. Anthony nodded: the name on the note matched the voice. LAMAR ...

"Well, I know about your meeting with Tex. I have been provided the details of your conversation. Spence, I would like to briefly address my concerns and then make a personal request. Can this conversation be kept strictly confidential? I certainly would not want the press to have any knowledge of our conversing during this strike. You can understand that, can't you?"

"Yes, sir, I can. No *real* information about what I am doing with regards to the strike has ever reached the press. I am sure that they think I'm in conference with members of the rosters of several teams, but they have only their own speculations as to what is going on behind the doors. No comment has come from my office or my clients. However, I will need to share all that I do regarding this matter with a very select few. I trust them implicitly to do what I ask. I hope that is acceptable. I went over that issue in great detail with Tex."

"I understand," he said. "Very well, then—I'll go ahead. I am well aware of the issues. I read your article in the *News* regarding the impending strike and agree with some of your opinions. But, whether I agree or disagree with your opinions, I respect your right to voice them and I respect your right to operate in the best interests of your clients. In other words, I realize that you're just doing your job as an attorney. So, here is my request. Before you decide to take any legal steps, which I anticipate you will, I would appreciate your advising Tex first. I do not intend to tell Tex about our conversation, though I am certain he will call me soon after he has talked with you. I realize that as a lawyer you can't give me too much of an alert: that would or could jeopardize your intentions. But I will tell you this. If I am provided enough of a window to deal with my people, I am confident whatever you're planning will become unnecessary. Again, even though it's no guarantee, I am sure you know that if you afford me time to initiate and influence a resolution, it should happen. No one wants to lose the season, Spence. No one wants to lose the new television contracts that will help pay the player salaries and potential bonuses."

"Sir, may I say this?" I asked.

"Go right ahead," he replied.

"Sir, these players have real financial concerns. There is an immediate need for adequate remuneration, *money now* for each player. They have their own responsibilities. That issue has been one the owners have flatly chosen to ignore. They have refused to adequately resolve or even address that issue on any level whatsoever. Even if you are successful, that issue remains, and that in itself is cause for the avenue of relief my guys will seek."

"Well," he said, "I'm confident that the owners will address everything. But all of what we are discussing is moot if the union doesn't cooperate. They seem to be immersed in their own vendettas. There will need to be some compromise."

"Yes, sir. Well … we've taken the union leaders and their vendettas into account."

"I believe it," he said. "So, we have an understanding?"

"I will honor your request, sir."

"Excellent. I was confident you would. Your alum advisor told me that your word was stronger than garlic breath. I believe I will rely on that. Spence, thank you. I appreciate your cooperation. I won't take up any more of your time. Have a nice day."

"Thank you, sir. Good-bye."

I hung up the phone and looked at the guys. They were completely floored by what had just transpired. I stared at each of them slowly, one by one, and whispered assertively, "This entire telephone conversation is not to leave this room without my authorization."

They looked at me, nodding their heads.

CHAPTER 24
No Looking Back

A view from Spencer Kopf

The players had been on strike for fifty-six days, and the union leadership had little, close to nothing, left in their tank. Our plan to attack their ineptness and lack of impartiality would ironically preserve their role in the union. They would be unable, however, to admit or acknowledge what was transpiring. We would force them to wait for the owners to react to our interrupting the labor talks. Wait, or let their leadership credentials disappear. A group of nearly twenty players came in and out of our office throughout the afternoon to confirm the following morning's 11:00 meeting. Each visitor wore an inscrutable countenance: he was either anxious or despondent or.... One player commented to Lisa, "Well, at least something will happen, one way or the other. It's about damn time."

The following morning Fred and I got up early and had breakfast at an IHOP in Richardson. We talked small for most of the meal, deliberately avoiding the topic and ticking seconds. At the office, around eight, I reviewed the legal drafts for the last time to have them fresh in my mind. I prepared to have the matter filed in federal court and would seek out Judge Robert M. Hill. Our office had someone posted downtown who would actually file the papers. We also had counsel at two other locations of competent jurisdiction to prevent the timely intervention of our adversary. Judge Hill's office was aware that we planned to file and would verify that a representative of our office was within earshot of the court clerk.

We had lived by my coach's alliterative aphorism: *Proper preparation promotes perfect performance.* The players, we were certain, had done the same. They started to arrive around ten. As usual, Lisa had thought ahead and had the deli prepare a table spread full of pastries, bagels, cheeses, and drinks. The giants in their business suits straggled about my office, catching crumbs in cocktail napkins; Noel, B. J., Fred, Anthony, and Norm were huddled around my desk, listening to me make the final arrangements. After placing the receiver back on its cradle, I turned to them and said, "Well, gentlemen, the stage is set. I guess it's time to open the curtain on our little play."

I rotated the phone, aiming the keypad away from me. B. J. nodded and snapped up the receiver. He dialed Robert Newhouse. "House" was the Dallas Cowboys' union player representative. He was also one of the nicest, down-to-earth guys you could ever wish to meet. House was respected and liked by his teammates and by the fans. I had recently represented his family for a corporate matter; he and his wife had been extremely professional and personable, business-minded and sincere. We were going to fill him in on what was about to be put in motion. We would be dealing directly with the player rep, just as the union had demanded. Just following their rules …

No answer. B. J. left a message at the union headquarters. Shortly after, the phone rang. I answered and greeted House warmly—to soften the blow of what I was about to have him deliver to Garvey. After the pleasantries, I said, "Robert, there are more than a few players in this league who have instructed my office to deal with the union leadership in less than peaceful terms. I am prepared to file a complaint that will require a legal ruling as to the inadequacy and lack of impartiality of the union's upper echelon. They will be temporarily restrained for up to fourteen days until a hearing takes place. After I complete my call, I will promptly notify Tex of our intentions. Both the union and owners will have three and half hours to rectify their differences, taking into consideration that there must be a significant cash remuneration by the owners to attempt to bring the players whole. If for some reason this is not accomplished, I suspect both sides will implode, and everyone can go on vacation several months early."

Robert responded politely and professionally: "Spence, can I talk with B. J.?"

"Robert, until these hours expire and we have determined what avenue we will take next, all communication will go only through my office. If any of the players are somehow contacted otherwise, they will forward calls to their attorney. Please contact the attorney for the union and advise him accordingly. In any case, I'm sorry I can't put you and B. J. together right now."

"I understand. Somebody here will get back to you," he said, unusually solemn, like the dial tone that followed him.

A short while later, Danny White, the starting quarterback for the Dallas Cowboys, called to speak with some of his teammates. They rebuffed the call. Then Dick Berthelsen called for our intentions. Several of the players and I had met Dick before. He was an attorney employed by the union. He cut to it: "You said you are seeking a restraining order for your clients. How are you going to post the bond to secure the TRO [temporary restraining order]? That bond will be huge."

My clients were listening in. I responded, "What bond? There won't be a bond. You guys, the union, and the owners are on strike. I am seeking a TRO to deter any conduct that could cause irreparable harm to my clients. A bond is set to provide economic protection from someone seeking a TRO—someone who could create imminent financial harm over the time frame of fourteen days or less. You guys have already imposed the ultimate economic harm on each other. There will not *be* a bond—and if there is one, it will be minimal. There *will* be a TRO put in place by late this afternoon. That is, unless there is a resolution to this matter, as I explained and described to Tex Schramm some time ago. This legal process exists outside the realm of your labor talks. I suggest you all spend your time resolving the issues. Excuse my forthrightness, but my clients are justified ..." The union's blinders had been removed, and I placed a call to Tex as promised.

Jerri Mote answered, and I said, "Jerri, is Mr. Schramm in? It's important that I speak with him. If he's not in, I can leave you a detailed message. Tex can call me back ... if he chooses."

"I'll have to have him get back with you. He is not available at this time," she said.

"Okay, please just tell him that I'm commencing a legal process. Someone affiliated with my office will be filing the action with a clerk in a little over three hours. I told Mr. Schramm that if I could, I would provide him some notice before I proceeded. Tell him that this is the best I can do. Please make sure he gets that message as expeditiously as possible because he pressed me pretty hard to do that for him, and I want to be sure he knows that I did."

"I'll be sure to let him know soon," she said.

The players sat, knees bouncing, fingernails chewed. Several of them were pacing the floor of my private waiting room like expectant fathers. A few sat impatiently on the couch and chairs in my office. Lisa suddenly sprang into my office and told me that Mr. Schramm was up front waiting for me. "He said he needed to speak with you right away ... what should I tell him?" I went behind my desk and asked her to escort him to my office. Tex walked quickly through the crowd of players in the waiting room; they parted like a wake to allow him to pass. He came through the door and immediately said in a surprisingly calm tone, "Spencer, you're filing a TRO? That will end the season. Are you *crazy*?"

"My doing what's right for my clients isn't what is going to end the season, Tex. You know that. You guys have had fifty-six days to work this stuff out."

"That's not our fault," said Tex, slightly more perturbed. "What they're asking for is flat out unreasonable."

"Tex, you're both unreasonable. If you guys don't step up and get money to these players now, you're right—the season probably will end. But look what can be accomplished: the union *will* talk with you now, if they haven't already."

"Spence, you realize if you do this, you're probably going to be nothing in this town?" He hadn't threatened me—he just believed it.

"Tex," I said respectfully, "you and Coach Landry know me by now. I have never betrayed your trust, regardless of the severity of the situation. And there have been more than a few: ask Coach. If I don't do this, I'll be nothing to myself."

"Very well," he said. "I do appreciate the heads-up. I guess—well, we might talk later." He wasn't happy with the situation, but he also realized he didn't have time to debate, especially not with all those players standing outside the door....

"If I'm not here, my office will be able to reach me," I said. He said nothing more and walked out.

The players peeked in, and I motioned for them with a gesture: a twitch of the fingers, because that was all that could move. I said, "Well, there goes my blue parking."

The nerves vanished; I regained mobility and leaned back in my chair. As I finished a sigh, Anthony quite astutely commented, "Hey, Spence, you're not in a popularity contest. We want money—they don't wanna pay. Of course they're gonna be pissed."

"No joke," added Fred.

All we could do now was wait.

Billy Joe: ... and still these guys are claiming they solved this strike. It's clear they know that is not true. The mediator was three thousand miles away, and they had to scramble to get a guy to sit in his place to deal with what our plan implemented. They were completely caught off guard and were then unprepared to deal with the problem. Joe, you were a player rep, right? The union leaders didn't know the strike was about to be settled without them!

Joe: I was a replacement rep, yeah. No, they didn't know anything. If they had, why'd the leaders send all of us home?

CHAPTER 25
Turmoil, Confusion, and Fear

A view from Joe DeLamielleure

The day started no differently than any other day at Camp DeLamielleure in Cleveland, Ohio. Each morning I would drive my kids to school and return home to discuss what my plans for the day should be with my wife, Gerri. You see, we have always been a team. Gerri and I have known each other since childhood. She is my best friend, confidant, mother of my children, and the one and only love of my life. So it was not unusual that I would share what was on my mind and vice versa during these trying times of the strike.

Today was different. When I was returning home from dropping my kids off, it really bothered me that I was not going to Brown's facilities to work out like I would every other season. It was extremely unsettling to me.

When I got home and started to share my thoughts with Gerri, I could tell that she was having the same feelings. She had a worried look on her face that was not typical. I became even more uneasy when I realized how worried she was.

She has always been my biggest cheerleader and greatest supporter. Almost every time I am down, she listens to me and does her best to try to pick my spirits up; but this time it was as if we were thinking the same thoughts, so instead of giving me the usual pep talk, she started commiserating with me.

"Joe," she started, "what are we going to do about the house in Charlotte, tell me, what? Almost all our savings were put into buying that house, and if we don't get some sizable funds in here soon, we could lose that house before we ever get to move in." Her voice was trembling with frustration and anger. Quite frankly, I couldn't blame her for feeling that way. But I had to be real with her because she would know if I wasn't. Gerri is not the type of person who will tolerate a spin on anything. She is a bottom-line person. She wanted an answer with a solution, or at the very least, a game plan that our family would follow.

"I understand where you're coming from," I said with a soft, reassuring tone. "Trust me, I do. I already have a job opportunity lined up with Hawk Industries if this crap with the union doesn't get resolved. But we are entering the seventh week of this strike, and something's gotta give soon or there won't be a season."

"Joe," she said, "I don't think we have the luxury to wait until next week to determine what we are going to do. We need to be seeking work opportunities now so we can start earning funds next week. Waiting could jeopardize the security of this family. I know you don't want to hear that. Believe me, I dreaded saying it. But I don't see any other alternative. That is, unless you have something already lined up with someone you know."

"I told you I do," I replied. "However, there still is hope that the strike will end soon. But in the event that it doesn't, I will start working at Hawk Industries next week. In the meantime, I'm gonna call Deek (Doug Dieken) to get the status of the strike, okay? Then, I'm going over to see DeLeone and see what he's up to."

"That's fine by me," she said, "but, please, don't just ask for a status. Press him for some details. They never tell us anything but for us to be patient. Try to find out what their plan is, and I don't mean just waiting around for the owners to quit."

"I will try, I promise. But I'm not counting on anything being different. The policy of the union is that all players have to go through their player reps to get any information."

"But they don't tell the reps anything, so how are we to find out what really is happening?"

With that, I decided to call Doug Dieken (the Cleveland Browns' union player representative) to get some answers now. I was anxious to say the least.

There was no answer. All types of scenarios danced in my head on what was happening in New York. I was tired of the nonanswer answers.

As I walked to the driveway, Gerri called out to me, "Joe, don't take the good car unless you will be back soon. Take the rent-a wreck because I have to run errands and get the kids, so I need the good car."

When we first went on strike, the car dealership that had loaned us a car for the year (for receiving season tickets) had taken their car back, leaving us with only one family car. Therefore, anticipating that the season would start up relatively soon, Gerri and I decided to just rent an old used car with payments due weekly until the season resumed.

Even though Gerri and I had some savings, we did not anticipate that the strike would last more than a few weeks. Our funds were running low, and panic was setting in. Unfortunately, that problem was not unique to us. Other players and their families were in significant distress and were unprepared to deal with it. That "Strike Fund" we were told about by Upshaw was nonexistent. What a song and dance that guy has. If he got paid a million dollars for each honest word he spoke, he would probably be on skid row or in a soup line somewhere. How in the hell did that two-faced disingenuous putz get in a leadership position in the union, and for that matter, stay there?

Our lives as we knew them were changing by the minute, and it was becoming frightening. Just think, at this point in time, we, as players, had no apparent control of our economic future, and that future was entrusted to people we were given little, if not zero, reason to trust and who had shown nothing but ineptness and unreliability in the way they were handling that trust.

I arrived home from my errands and found Gerri with the twins, Todd and Alison. Since Gerri always took care of the finances, I asked her to look over things and let me know where we stood, and I took over playing with the kids. It was then when I got an unexpected phone call from Doug Dieken.

"Hey, Joe, it's Deek," he said.

"What's up?" I replied.

"Look, Joe, apparently there's a meeting being held in New York with the union leadership and the player reps tomorrow, which I didn't find out about until now. Problem is, I can't possibly go. So, I was hoping that you could go in my place and find out what's going on and represent us there. The union will pay your way there and pick up the hotel expenses. Can you do it?"

"What's up about this meeting? What's it for?" I asked.

"I'm not sure," he said. "But I was told it was important and that they were hopeful something might break this week. That's all they told me. Either way, I've got to find someone to go, and I'd hoped it could be you since you've been around the league longer than most of the guys, and they look up to you."

"Who do I need to talk with to make the travel arrangements and hotel reservations?" I asked.

"Just call the NFLPA office and tell them that you are substituting for me and they will set it up for you. Thanks for doing this, Joe," he said.

"No problem," I responded. "I am more than curious to find out what really is happening and what the status of the season is, if you know what I mean."

"Well, I can't think of a better way to find out. Let me know what you find out. Oh, and by the way, thanks for stepping up, Joe," he said.

"You bet."

As I hung up the phone, I felt a strange sense of anxiety. *Maybe,* I thought, *maybe I'll find out what really is going on. Maybe I'll get some straight answers with some details as well.*

I was excited at the prospect of finally getting some answers as to what was going on. When I rejoined my wife and told her what had just happened, she was relieved at the possibility of getting some answers as well. She is very logical and levelheaded, so the two of us sat down and started making a list of the questions I needed to ask to make sure that I got an informative, satisfactory response. Then, as usual, she picked out my clothes and helped me pack. Is there anything that gal can't do?

I arrived in New York at LaGuardia Airport and took a taxi to the hotel to meet the rest of the player reps. The ride to the hotel seemed as long as the flight, as traffic was heavy and I was very anxious to get on with what I had come there to do. I realized then, as I do now, that I did not have the mindset of a patient man when it came to these circumstances.

When I arrived at the hotel, I checked into my room, notified the union office of my arrival, and was told to await their call. None came. With that, I resigned myself to the fact that I needed to take matters into my own hands and attempt to find out what was going on from the other reps there. That became more difficult than I had originally assumed.

It appeared that the union leadership had notified a select few that there was not going to be a meeting that day after all. Apparently, they said, everything was on hold. Since I did not personally know many of the reps well and the union leadership was limiting accessibility to them—and restricting information regarding the status of the strike's negotiations to only them—players, including myself, were becoming extremely frustrated and agitated.

Then, as I was sitting in the lobby awaiting some kind of word, one of the player reps came over to those congregated near the bar and advised them that there was not going to be a meeting with the player reps that day. Furthermore, the rest of us were then informed that the NFL season would in all probability end unless the union constituency would agree to accept what was already in place by the owners with few or no changes pertaining to the other union issues of contention. They said there had been some talk of some small token of money as an incentive to get the players to capitulate, but that alleged possibility was apparently no longer available as far as the owners were concerned.

What kind of bullshit was this? Travel all this way to be told that nothing had been or would be accomplished and that the season would probably come to an end unless we succumbed? What was this important meeting we were to have before I left balmy Cleveland? What progress was being made by the union leadership? What spin were they about to unleash on our mostly naive membership?

As I sat pensively on the large greeting couch by the revolving doors, I was approached by a group of younger player reps, who queried whether I would like to join them for some dinner and some exotic dancing at a nearby strip joint. Not exactly enticing to an old-fashioned, happily married Catholic and father of four.

I reassessed my position and decided to return home to my family and deal with those issues I could address, not those I couldn't. Time was not something I could afford to waste. I called Gerri, and we decided it was best that I come home.

The next morning arrived. Tom DeLeone, our eleven-year veteran and All-Pro Bowl center, and I had planned to go over to Hawk Industries to see when we could start. There was no other choice. We needed to earn money, and football didn't appear to be an option that would satisfy our economic needs. Based upon what we had been told, even if we were to go back to playing soon, we would all be out the money for the time we had already missed, and that money would have to be made up another way.

Just before we were intending to go over to our friend's company, I received a telephone call from Mike Brown of the Cincinnati Bengals. Mike's dad, Paul Brown, was the former owner and head coach of the Cleveland Browns and the current owner of the Bengals.

I didn't know Mike personally, but he apparently knew of me and had called for a specific purpose. He called to tell me that the owners were not going to give in to the demands of the union leadership. He further indicated that he respected me as a player and as a leader of my team. He suggested that I consider crossing the line and return to work as a statement of leadership for my teammates. It would also serve as a voice against the inadequate and incompetent union leadership.

Although the phone call was short, it was a further indication that the owners were not going to resolve any of the issues with the union regarding benefit packages or economic remuneration. It was either go back to work as before (or even worse) or get another job.

Tom and I decided to have lunch and discuss our options before talking with the other guys.

Tom and I had a nice lunch and an even better discussion. We spoke with our friend about working for his company now, instead of waiting for the off-season, to facilitate our shortfall in income. All went well. He was great about it. I decided that I would go home and spend the time with Gerri since I knew I would be working next week.

In my past experiences, I had learned to always prepare for the unexpected to happen, even though the probability was remote or even close to impossible. That is true especially in the category of a sporting event. You know what I mean. A last-minute basket from a nearly full court with the clock running out to win the game by one point. Leading a team by thirteen points with less than one minute to play in a football game, only to have the other team score on a long pass, recover an onside kick, and connect on a "Hail Mary" pass to win.

Well, you could have knocked me over with a feather when I heard that the strike was over and the teams were providing us players "Money Now" checks to return to work. Yeah, right, and the Pope will be Jewish on Monday. Not only that, but the "Money Now" check I would receive would be the largest check I would get as a player at one time, ever.

Now, at the time, I didn't know what had happened to the owners that caused such a huge, unlikely turnaround in their *etched-in-stone* position. I did know this much: the union leadership had absolutely nothing to do with it. When the union leadership was queried as to what had happened, all they said was that it didn't matter how it happened—it only mattered that it *had* happened. I quickly recalled how adamant Mike Brown's tone was when he spoke to me about the owners' resolve. The entire scenario of that phone call would make no sense in the wake of a settlement just several hours later; the owners had suddenly shifted from steadfast to soft. Why?

It was clear that some outside source had forced the capitulation of this labor strike, and the union leadership was merely along for the ride when that happened. Heck, the arbitrator, Kagel, wasn't even there when the agreement was apparently reached. Why wasn't a delay sought in the negotiations until Kagel arrived? Because there wasn't time. Instead of calling Kagel back, the two warring parties—under the impassable, imposed, and invisible time constraint—were pressed to recruit a pinch hitter, a guy named Paul Martha. Naturally, nobody on either side would ever fess up that they had lost all control.

I will say this: a second slingshot had hit its mark to bring an apparently unbeatable foe to its knees. No one saw it coming, and no one saw it land. But everyone heard the thud. Now that's what I call a miracle finish.

Billy Joe: House ... House has never let me down, man. Not then as rep, not now as a friend—not ever....

CHAPTER 26
Behind Union Doors

A view from Robert Newhouse

Although the conversation between Dick Berthelsen and Spence probably lasted under two minutes, the aftershock from that phone call upon the union leadership seemed to last an eternity. The moment Berthelsen informed them of what had crossed the phone lines, the members of the NFLPA brain trust were paralyzed. To the man, they were completely unprepared for what had just happened; they appeared totally helpless, desperate.

As Berthelsen left the room of union advisors and other union leaders, Upshaw exclaimed through the doorway, "Fix this quick, or it's gonna be a fuckin' mess." Berthelsen walked toward me briskly, and in mid-stride he said, "Do you know anyone who can talk some sense into this guy? What about one of the players he has in his group? You should explain to them that we are at the eleventh hour, and that the timing of this couldn't be worse: that it will damage any chance of settlement—that it will cost us the season.... Doesn't he realize that he's just helping the owners by doing this?"

"Dick," I said, "I didn't know any of this was going on. In fact, I only know of two of my teammates that are in the group that Spence is representing. But believe me when I tell you, Billy Joe DuPree is a respected leader. He wouldn't have taken these steps, along with the others involved, unless they believed in what they were doing. And I know Spence. I know him pretty well. He may be arrogant at times, and he may appear to be overconfident, cocky even, overly aggressive, but he's extremely devoted to his clients. And he's just going to seek the best possible result for *them.* He wouldn't do anything as drastic as this unless he had examined the options thoroughly, from every possible angle. They've sought out some serious legal help, I'll bet. Some seriously talented legal minds have looked this over, something as profound as this, you can be sure. He is not the kind of guy who will play poker unless he knows for certain that he has a winning hand. I just don't think he's the kind of person who would try an all-out bluff in a matter as serious as this; that's not his way."

"Well," he responded curtly, "see what you can do to get him to hold off. We need to resolve this without outside interference. It shows weakness within our group, and that could hurt our leverage with the owners and weaken our union. Maybe we should get Danny to talk to—who is it?—DuPree, to see if he can talk some sense into him."

"I'll see what I can do," I said. "But I don't think it would be wise using Danny to get these guys to change their minds. He may be our quarterback when we play, but he is not someone the guys will listen to about legal matters and career moves. They look at Danny as being a corporate man, and not necessarily one of them. Danny has a high opinion of himself, which doesn't sit well with some of our teammates."

"Danny seems to want to try," said Berthelsen. "He believes he can make a difference. Let him try. I need to get back inside and see what alternative plan we can develop to deal with this fiasco. Time's short, Robert. Let me know what you are able to do. Please keep me informed."

With that, Berthelsen turned and disappeared behind the conference room doors. He was pissed. The union's higher echelon could be heard shouting obscenities through the walls. Every few minutes, Gene Upshaw would stick his head out and instruct one of the office personnel to contact one lawyer or another. Once a lawyer was on the line, the secretary would forward the call to the conference room. Each time he stuck his head out to get in touch with another attorney, the more impatient and angrier he became. Upshaw apparently was unhappy with the commentary he was receiving from his legal team. As for me, I resigned myself to the fact that I had been relegated to reconnect with Billy Joe DuPree and attempt to get him and his group to cease and desist from going forward with any legal action against the union leadership.

Once I reached Spencer's office, I was informed that no player would be granted access to discuss any legal matters with union representatives until the strike had been resolved. It was made unequivocally clear that all communications would need to go through their legal counsel.

At that point, Danny White insisted on calling Billy Joe directly. When he realized that he could not reach him, he called Spencer's office. Spencer reluctantly answered the call and quickly rebuffed Danny's rhetoric. He politely but directly notified Danny that Danny was not privy to the depths of what had been going on and what was going on—Danny must have been misinformed about the resolve of the maverick group of players. Spence then politely but firmly ended the call. Being curt with Danny didn't sit well with Spence. He liked Danny, but given the circumstances, there was no other choice.

Up until the phone call from B. J. to me, the progress in the labor talks between the parties was pretty much nonexistent. The owners and the union leadership were no closer on day fifty-six than they were on day one. The pressure was mounting. In fact, the arbitrator, Sam Kagel, had left the labor talks on the forty-seventh day, recommending that the parties reflect on what they were seeking in hopes of drawing the parties closer together. I think he was just plain tired of hearing the same bullshit from both sides.

But now was different. Now, the owners would be faced with serious consequences (unbeknownst to the union leadership), and the union leadership, if the truth came out, would appear to be ineffectual and incompetent. Apart from those present who were within the union leadership, those party to the owner's strike committee (and the individual owners themselves), and those players associated with the group represented by Spence, no one else would be aware of the truth. The public and the press would only know what was provided in the releases and interviews.

It became more and more evident that the owners were far from pleased about what was transpiring. But funny as it may seem, the union leadership's arrogance had kept them blind to their surroundings. They were blind to the fact that this little coup d'état had swiftly overpowered the owners (in a way the union leaders never could) to such a large extent that the owners were in a more tenuous position: the mere exposure of the union leadership's incompetence to the public and its membership, or the financial woes of the union rank and file, would be nothing compared to the impact on the owners. But it was clear by the conduct of the union leadership that it was more important to them that they save face rather than reach an amicable settlement with the owners (whether it was due to the union's efforts or not).

Time raced. Approximately thirty to forty-five minutes elapsed before Berthelsen reappeared in the main waiting area with Upshaw. Their faces wore scowls, and their words were choppy and abrupt. Although the news they were about to share was promising to those of us who were waiting, it must have felt like eating crow to them.

"This strike could be resolved within the hour," grumbled Berthelsen.

"What happened?" I asked.

"I don't have all the information just yet," he said. "When I do, I'll *share* it with you. What I came to tell you is that the settlement of this strike is imminent."

"How did you guys get all this done within such a short time frame? Last night you guys canceled the player rep meeting, and told the guys to go home if they wanted because the arbitrator wasn't here yet. You went from no movement at all to a possible settlement in the past *half-hour*? Now another arbitrator is here? What's going on? Hell, this new guy hasn't even had time to go to the bathroom. What gives?"

"That isn't the issue," said Berthelsen. He was poorly hiding what was really happening. "What is important is that we are close to reaching agreeable terms that should satisfy all parties concerned."

He retired to the conference room to confer with Upshaw and his other cronies.

If what Berthelsen just announced was true, then why the hell were they not celebrating all over the place? Why was there no glad-handing, backslapping, and bragging by Upshaw? What was truly happening behind those closed doors? Then reality sank in. Things started popping when B. J. called me. Whatever B. J.'s group was doing or planned on doing had utterly turned the world upside down for the owners and the union leadership. What made matters worse was that it appeared that neither side had an adequate answer available to them to either negate or even stall the rebellion's apparently perfectly choreographed attack. This wasn't a stalemate; it looked like checkmate.

The union leadership wasn't behind closed doors trying to come up with an alternative plan; it was too late for that. They were in there planning damage control. What spin could they use if the maverick plan failed? What spin could they use if the maverick plan had some success? Did the union leaders even have enough time to spin?

Whatever credibility Upshaw and his group had had with me was now at an all-time low. They didn't hide their emotions well, and their claim to know what was going on, when it was so obvious that they didn't, made them look foolish. Looking back, it is incomprehensible to me that Upshaw, Berthelsen, and the others ever led the union. The truth of their leadership tenure would be forthcoming and be exposed for what it was.

CHAPTER 27
Truth and Courage Carry the Day

A view from Spencer Kopf

It was now clear to the players that control had shifted dramatically. Our conversations with both strike talk participants had determined the terms of the outcome of one major issue. The owners and the union knew that there would have to be considerable money available to each player upon resolution of the strike or there would be no resolution. One problem, however, remained: to accomplish a settlement, the union would need to abandon some of their earlier unrealistic yet still uncompromised demands. It was almost pitiable: the new arbitrator had no clue what was happening—submission was the only option. The union and the owners were back at the table under pressure to resolve their differences.

As the clock approached the second hour since the meeting with Tex, the players grew more restless. Most of the guys realized that both sides would need to capitulate immediately and coequally to each other's six-week-old demands to reach an agreement in the allotted time. When I began to pack my briefcase to head downtown and join my friend, a call came in from Tex: "Spencer, progress is being made, but we need more time."

I responded politely, but matter-of-factly, "Tex, I am truly sorry, but that's not an option I can recommend to my clients ... not under any circumstance. Your legal advisors know perfectly well why that option is unavailable. Please excuse my directness, but we're going to proceed as previously specified ... we *will* file in a city of competent jurisdiction. Your lawyers will explain why if they haven't already."

After that call, the tension had made the air in the room thick, nearly unbreathable. The players needed to know why I could not accommodate the owners' request for delay. Maybe we *should* give the owners some space—so they can work things out with the union, Spence. One of the younger guys *demanded* we call Tex back. He approached my desk to have me make (or was it make me have?) the call, but I remained calmly seated in my blue-leather, high-backed chair and ignored his defiance. Then this unnamed sprout attempted to come around to my side. Fred and Norm intercepted gracefully, as if warned by some shared sense, some mutual precognition. The boy's countenance was curled in anger. The stare-down between that boy and their human wall was the longest fifteen seconds in my memory. They fortunately had not yet touched each other. The incident was about to become a very heated debate or, I began to fear, much worse. Instead, civility won the day, as did preparation: the self-appointed leaders of our group had privately discussed what to do should this situation arise. They reminded the player—whose every in- and exhalation was still violent and perceptible—that they had agreed to democratically decide what to do. And, to the man, they agreed that the path I was about to take was the only path available. Tex would not be called. The young player had ceased to hyperventilate, and the wall became two men again.

I said, "Listen up." The din of overlapping conversations continued. "Please," I said, more firmly. I waited patiently for them to quiet down. Noel, Norm, and B. J. canvassed the room, seeking compliance. When it was silent, I said, vehemently, "Thank you. The entire purpose of The Plan is to remove actual and potential current control from the owners. We cannot grant the owners or the union leadership any grace period. They will use their superior force of influence and economic power to regain control during any armistice. This live, true, and actual threat of a two-week, *uncontrolled* restraining order of all parties levels the playing field temporarily. And it is an advantage we *must* maintain. Does everyone understand that?" All were silent. "Patience, fellas. We're almost home. Otherwise, Tex would not have made that call just now; that call was just Plan A."

The players seemed cautiously optimistic. However, they were still throwing around "fuck" like gangsters in a Scorsese film. Then, sooner than expected, Tex called back.

"Spencer, there is an agreement. It should be reduced to writing momentarily. It will resolve the strike. The collective bargaining agreement shall run up to the 1987 season. The owners shall disperse funds to each player based upon their years in the league as a settlement incentive—that will satisfy the concerns you had previously spelled out to me. And the media should know shortly: the acting arbitrator will confirm the agreement in a media release, which should also happen very soon." Tex was good at stating things so that they sounded like your idea. Of course, they would handle the media....

"Thank you for the call, Tex. Obviously, I will only refrain from going forward once I have received official confirmation from the arbitrator ... and only if the 'Money Now' package is consistent with what was previously discussed. But based upon what you have just told me, I am sincerely glad this matter has been amicably resolved."

Every word of the conversation had wound the players closer and closer to the desk. I hung up the phone, and the spring-loaded mass exploded in elation like the omnidirectional streams of a firecracker. Then confirmation came, again sooner than anticipated, and the scene repeated itself around the nucleus that was my desk. They were so excited that some of them just sat down from exhaustion. Others, the ones who had just crawled from personal quicksand, left the room with damp eyes to call loved ones.

I leaned back in my chair holding my hands behind my head as I enjoyed the scenery. Who would have believed it? I felt like actor Harry Carey's vice president at the end of *Mr. Smith Goes to Washington* as he watches the Senate chambers erupt in pandemonium.

Moments can be dwelled upon; they can be remembered and examined. But that last moment, while exhilarating, was transient and fleeting, like a sonic boom. In a flash, only the founders of our group remained. The rest had rushed home, under the smoke screen of the celebration, to be with their families.

Lisa ran to the front to answer the phone. She buzzed to tell me that my "big brother" was on line two. I raised my right index finger to my lips and lifted the receiver: "Hello."

"Hello, Brother Kopf."

"Hello, sir, it's good to hear from you," I said.

"I called to thank you for honoring your commitment. As I expected, a lot of people are a bit miffed, but, as they say, time heals *most* wounds. What's more important, Spence, is that there is peace in the game."

"That's right, sir. But it sure wasn't easy," I replied.

"It wasn't easy. But remember, the important things in life aren't supposed to come easy, are they? Spence, Brother Huebner, Jack Haaker, and your AA were right about you. I want you to know that you should be proud—really proud," he said.

"Sir, coming from you that means more than you know. Thank you."

"Spence, you have a great rest of the day. You earned it. And enough with that *sir.* You call me Lamar. AEKDB. Take care." Then, in the same ethereal way he had vanished into the crowd the last time I had seen him, he gingerly hung up his phone. Anthony Dickerson, who knew Lamar Hunt from his playing years at SMU, turned to the rest of us and said, "That is one amazing dude." The few of us knew that already, but I was glad one of them said it out loud.

They all decided to grab a beer together (Noel would have a Sprite) before heading home. I told them I'd meet them downstairs, and they left.

I sat there and suddenly snapped out of my calm for a moment—I suddenly felt overwhelmed. It hits you after the ball leaves the park how important your swing was; you sense it only as you round the bases in solitude. Your timing, aim, and luck were crucial to your little victory. And, ironically, if done correctly, you don't even feel the ball leave the bat—you feel a home run when you've felt nothing at all. I must have sat behind that desk a few minutes before B. J. abruptly poked his head in and said, "You all right, Spence?"

I glanced up from the desk. "Yeah, B. J. I'm good."

He said, "Come on. Let's get a beer."

I sighed, and thought, *Time to run the bases.* Guess who got stuck with the tab?

The next morning, I dropped off Fred at the airport. I arrived at the office around ten o'clock. Just as I entered, Lisa handed me a message that read, "Chet Simmons, Commissioner of USFL. Please return call after 2:00, New York time."

Lisa added, "Dave Smith called and said if you didn't call him, you were dogmeat."

"Fine, would you get him on the phone while I get the information from Pete Vouras about the Chateaubriand Restaurant? Oh, yeah, if you can, reschedule my four o'clock set for this afternoon—that would be good. Try and move it up to two. I've got to go to McKinney to see the court coordinator for County Court One. One of my neighbors has a son in need of a lawyer. I'd give you the information, but I don't have it yet. It's a pro bono matter."

"You know you're supposed to charge people, remember?" she asked.

"Well, the family's in a bind; he's not quite twenty."

"Spence, you are too much of a soft touch, you know what I mean?" She excused herself to answer the telephone. It was Dave Smith.

Lisa rang through, "Spence, Dave is on line two."

I lifted the receiver and greeted Dave. "Hello, Dave, what's cooking?"

"*You* apparently. Hell of a job, little guy. And you're still healthy. Not bad. So, what's the encore?" He laughed.

"Cute. Just remember, you're responsible for all this," I temporized.

"You still haven't answered my question...."

"Well, we're going to have a gathering at the house for the guys and all those wonderful people like you who didn't run away or pretend not to know me."

"Isn't it cool when the bad guys know there are reinforcements in the wings? It must have been fun," he said.

"Yeah, sure, it was a blast. A bagful of laughs, Dave."

"Hey, this is just the beginning. You've got all that new stuff on the horizon. Don't you think? The USFL could be a real alternative."

"It's possible."

"Do you have time for lunch?"

"Only if you're not buying. I don't want any more sandwiches out of a vending machine—"

"Fine, I'll come by your office in an hour. Oh, by the way, do my guys get to write about what happened in your office yesterday?"

"Not a chance—no way," I replied firmly.

"I understand. It was pretty damn amazing, though. Shame ..." he said. "All right, buddy, I'm hungry. See you soon."

"Do me a favor, don't speed. I don't wanna deal with any more traffic tickets for friends."

"You got it," he snapped, chortling.

I hung up the phone and caught the light over Noel's line flashing. He was paging from his office. I picked up the phone, touched his line, and before the receiver had reached my ear, Noel had already begun to say, "Chief, the New Jersey Generals of the United States Football League is on the phone—line one."

"Can you take a message? I need to go down the hall first."

Noel responded briskly, "Chief, you need to hold junior in your pants. Take the call now."

"I've got it. Line one?" Jesus, I didn't even have time to take a piss.

"Line one ..." Noel repeated. I pressed the button, and Noel was gone.

"Hello, this is Spencer," I said.

"Hello, Spencer. This is Chuck Fairbanks of the New Jersey Generals. We met while I was at Oklahoma. Well, I'd like to visit with you. Got a minute?"

EPILOGUE

by Billy Joe DuPree

Why There Was No Other Choice

Back on July 30, 1982, I was quoted in a newspaper article in the *Dallas Morning News*[9] regarding the deplorable manner in which the management of my team had conducted themselves during employment contract negotiations. Here is how the article read and how I was quoted:

> *"They had added a little to my contract this year," DuPree said, "but nothing compared to what they gave guys who were watching in their mother's arms while I was here making this a better place. In regard to what has transpired in the off season, I am unhappy. Guys who have been here two or three years and haven't played much are making more than me.*
>
> *"I'm disappointed they haven't tried to take care of me as well as I've taken care of them. My situation comes down to*

9   Myers, "Dutton's Disgusted."

one of two choices: retire or walk out. At the present time, I'm considering neither. Nice guys never come in first. If I was a complete bleep they would do something about it."

DuPree has never been able to catch up from what he terms a bad rookie contract, which he negotiated himself after being drafted on the first round in 1973.

"From day one as a rookie, I never got what I was looking for," he said. "I've always been (...). The Cowboys are a great business organization, but that doesn't say anything about the personality of it."

Other teammates voiced their disdain with the management in that article just as forcefully as I. John Dutton, one of the most respected players on our roster, was quoted as follows:

"My opposition before was to Ed Garvey. Now, I realize ballplayers are just trying to take care of themselves. I worked my butt off for the Cowboys and got nothing in return. Striking is the only way to get things done. I was naïve to think the Cowboys take care of their people. Common business sense says you take care of your good people. If you got unhappy people, you're not going to win.

"They don't want to give up a dime. I know I deserve more money, and they know it, too. I will survive. No one will break me."

Doug Cosbie, my heir apparent at tight end, a good guy and excellent family man, was covered as well:

"They said they don't give signing bonuses to players who haven't made All-Pro. But they gave one to Kurt Petersen. It's funny,

because we have the same agent (Spencer Kopf), and they told
him two different things," Cosbie said. "I'm not impressed with
the business end of this organization, with the way they handle
players. I'm not happy with the management end of it.

"That's a big part of it, because they keep telling you this
is a business. Next year, I won't negotiate. I'll tell them what I
want. I won't play out my option. I've explained that to them.
I'll leave before I play out my option."

Cosbie said he would go into private business and be happy
making $25,000 if that's all his boss could afford to pay him.
But, he said he couldn't be happy in football not earning what
he thinks he's worth and what he believes the Cowboys could
afford to pay him.

For years, the management of professional football has taken
advantage of the fact that the athletes in their sport were virtually
unable to shop their wares to other organizations, unable to seek
proper compensation and proper benefits. After reading the July 11,
1982 article that Spencer had written, I knew that he had completely
and accurately analyzed the dilemma of the professional football
player, as well as the nuances and patterns of the owners during
labor talks. He poignantly pointed out, until free agency was fought
for in the courts, player leverage was limited at best. We all saw
the inadequacies of the union management, but we saw no way
around them.

So we asked.

The answer was direct. The popular KISS method: Keep It Simple,
Stupid. Spence determined that, based on the owners' previous
conduct during negotiations, the owners would drag out any talks just
to imply weakness and impotence in the union leadership and power

and control in themselves. The owners could not sense their own vulnerability; they were blinded by their arrogance. And they allowed themselves to be led unwittingly into a situation in which control of negotiations was no longer within their grasp. They obviously missed how their lack of control could drastically affect their bottom line.

I carefully reviewed all the options available to my teammates and my constituents in the league. We would lay in wait as if we were waiting for the union to breach the owners' walls. We knew by past performance and by the tone of the owners that was not going to happen anytime soon, not at this union's pressing. When the time presented itself, we would strike our own stance for fair compensation and fair play—and damn the consequences for all concerned. Not for revenge. Not out of arrogance. Not for ego and not to humiliate. Free agency would be the epitome of "what goes around comes around" for the owners. But that would be ten years hence.

This one day, we had one small shot to accomplish something that had yet to be done in the history of professional football. The crack in the vault was small, but it was forced open wide enough to get us in. My "Money Now" check (approximately $110,000) created by The Plan was the most money I received at one time as a player, ever. Spence's theory made sense—and his theory made cents. We are all proud we had the common temerity to see it through.

Today's players reap what the players before free agency sowed. It is time for them to share with those in need, with those players and their families who made sacrifices so that the future players of the game wouldn't have to.

Tony: You really squeezed them into a corner …

Billy Joe: Yeah, we did.… But we weren't given a choice. They set this up, and Spence found the corner they'd squeezed themselves into.

Tony: No, you really got them, B. J. How can we get them over the barrel like that again?

Joe: We let them know that the jig is up now. The time of empty promises is over. The world knows part of the story, and in a way that should be enough. I mean, a $28 million punitive neon sign should be enough for this Director Smith to know that he needs to clean house to fix this problem, damn it. He keeps them! He *keeps* them! But the light of your story, B. J., just shows how inept these guys are and have always been. And how insensitive they are to the well-being of the players, some of whom are starving now, players who can't walk a hundred yards without stopping to pause 'cause of bad knees and bad backs and bad memories of cortisone shots. It's time to let the world know that this ain't nothing new. The world needs to learn how cheap the union talk is, and needs to start demanding that any talk be backed up by real action; they need to—

Tony: Joe?

Billy Joe: Hello? Joe?

Tony: His grandson must have gotten hold of the phone again. Maybe just lost the battery.

Billy Joe: You have grandkids, Tony?

Tony: Sure do.

Billy Joe: Well, for their sake, and for all our guys and their grandkids, DeMaurice Smith better do something to back up his promises, or he'll have more than guys like Joe to answer to …

Tony: Is there some time next week when we can chat, B. J.? I've got a suit in the works that could really use your support …

Billy Joe: Go ahead and ring me anytime. We'll set something up.

Tony: Adios.…

Tony Davis and Joe DeLamielleure are seasoned NFL veterans and players' union members. They, like most retired players, know quite well what the lay fan knows little about—after all, they lived it. They know that the leaders of the players' union time and again since 1977 have represented their members in a manner that can at best be described as ineffective. It has taken thirty-one years for any retribution, if not for the maltreatment that they had received while they were active players, then for the civil transgression their union is now paying for.

The situation, however, is much more grim than Joe's first reaction let on: this $28 million victory is a small one. Sure, the jury had "made a statement" with that sum: a mere $7.1 million were actual damages; punitive damages were a whopping $21 million. But Tony was right: the union would pay, not the individual leaders who actually ordered retired players scrambled into anonymity while the leaders cashed it in only for active players and Player's, Inc. As it happens, Richard Berthelsen (current counsel and former acting executive director of the NFLPA) admits that they only cashed it in for the current players; he opines that it is because the union leaders are "paid out of revenues generated by active players."[10] Well, not only did the jury find otherwise—after all, the NFLPA leaders sure made cash out of retired players when they purposely refused to acknowledge them on an incredibly successful,

----

10   Horwitch, "Company Set Up by SAG's Allen Under Fire."

money-generating video game; but Berthelson seems to forget that regardless of player performances and video game sales, NFLPA leaders get paid their obscenely large salaries no matter what, salaries that they, of course, set through their direction and influence.

And have they been paid! In 2005–06, Doug Allen, the former assistant director of the NFLPA and 1994 founder of Players, Inc., earned $466,281. The next year, he was paid $1.9 million. His wife, Pat, the former C.O.O. of Players Inc., doubled her salary to over $600 thousand. And Gene Upshaw, the NFLPA executive director, raked in nearly $7 million.[11] Anyone see a conflict of interest here? These people hold dichotomous positions: they are union leaders and Players, Inc., board members and in all probability have or had ownership in that company as well. Why does Players, Inc., exist at all if its duties are already assumed by leadership positions in the NFLPA; why are these people paid through two sources, out of the same funds, for virtually doing one job? They will argue that marketing just isn't something that the NFLPA handles, and thus, they started a company to handle the marketing. But this most recent lawsuit shows the conflict that should be staring everyone in the face: the reason they didn't fulfill the fiduciary duty to the retired, scrambled players, as required by their NFLPA positions, was that they had an interest in making money for Players, Inc., and its leaders, themselves. Furthermore, Players, Inc., also receives annual revenue from the NFL Internet and sponsorship agreements, for doing absolutely nothing.[12] Why doesn't all of this money flow directly into the NFLPA for the benefit of union members only? Because, one could assume, it has to flow through Players, Inc., for the benefit of those who run that company—naturally.

---

11   Ibid.
12   Masteralexis, Barr, and Hums, *Principles and Practice of Sport Management*, p. 417.

The union intended to have a leadership board fairly represent its members; it did not intend for the union leadership to throw extravagant all-expenses-paid trips for extended weekend parties to Hawaii, use thousands of dollars of money derived from union sources (which includes Players, Inc.) for a self-aggrandized state-of-the-art fireworks display, and then go around voting to deprive needy union members the most basic economic assistance for physical disabilities. One retired union member's request for assistance was being sought after seven spinal surgeries had been confirmed and verified proof of no income earned by the applicant had been properly submitted to the union leadership for review. The union board voted nay for the disability benefits.

The recently elected executive director, attorney DeMaurice Smith, attended the most recent NFLPA meetings in Hawaii while campaigning for that position, so he is well aware of what is going on—or should be. The assistant to Mr. Smith released Smith's biography, where it states that he had presented the union with a "comprehensive plan [having assembled] roughly a dozen advisers" to help him to prepare: Wall Street financiers, labor lawyers, and sports licensing experts. "His goals include increasing health care and opportunities for former and current players and he believes: 'the union has both a moral and business obligation to retired players.'"[13] Such statements are certainly pleasant to the ears of those retired players who are in need of some kind of hope—that is, if those words of faith and encouragement are beyond mere rhetoric. Unfortunately, despite only being on the job for less than a year, it is unequivocally clear that those statements by the new executive director barely transcend the emptiness of politically cooked promises. Like the best of such word play, they appear and sound heartfelt, but his actions indicate that these words are apparently disingenuous.

13   Wilner, "New NFLPA Exec Working Without Contract."

By permitting and welcoming the assistance of the previous union leadership to his regime—leaders who were besmirched in open court by a judge and a jury of their peers for breaching a fiduciary duty, leaders who led a failed strike in 1987 resulting in union decertification, leaders who were lame in 1982—Director Smith has taken a very dubious first step in accomplishing his goals. By keeping them and their committee members, or simply leaving some in place, at best he has ignored their past unconscionable conduct, and at worst he has validated it.

The money managed and intended to be managed by the union leadership should belong to the union for union purposes and for union members. The strongest sense of fiduciary duty befalls all union leaders when they are installed in their positions of office. Those positions come veiled in a shroud of trust. But it's been torn.

His assistant mentioned that Mr. Smith researched and sought expert advice before he made his presentation to the active player reps. Smith had acknowledged meeting at length with the current union leadership, committee members, and others involved with the day-to-day operations of the NFLPA and Players, Inc. He leads all of us to believe that he has conducted a thorough, due-diligence preparation for his new post of employment. So, Mr. Smith, how do you justify the roster of people who should have been summarily terminated at the NFLPA upon your election, but were instead retained?

In a recent radio interview with host and former Buffalo Bill Jeff Nixon, Tony Davis reported that when he asked former president of the NFLPA, Troy Vincent, how they let Gene Upshaw have so much power, Mr. Vincent, like Mr. Smith, took the platitudinous route: "I prefer to think about the future," he said, "not dwell on the past."[14] Well, as we mentioned before, those who are unaware of their past are doomed to repeat it—and willful ignorance, if we are going to use platitudes, is not

14   Jeff Nixon Sports Report.

a good thing. Upshaw's position as executive director was not supposed to be one of unbridled power—in fact, the position does not even have a vote. But without any checks and balances, Upshaw did have the power to hire and appoint whomever he wanted—and he did. It sure seems, with the election of Mr. Smith and his subsequent ridiculous decision to leave certain employees employed and committee members on board, that bad history is back.

A complete restructuring of the NFLPA will be required. This should include revisions and amendments to the constitution and bylaws that properly and adequately protect the sanctity and integrity of the union; there need to be enough checks and balances to ensure these protections and prohibit conflicts of interest; there should be no possibility of self-enrichment or unreasonable financial gain by any union or union-affiliated employee (like those of Players, Inc., for example). In other words, the diversion of money from union members must end, and this must be a protection afforded by the NFLPA Constitution.

*There is no longer the luxury of waiting until next year. Another labor strike is on the horizon, with no apparent viable foundation of leadership in place to effectuate the needed results. Now is the time that the new union leadership and its active and retired members should relate to each other in the manner and spirit in which the union was originally founded: **All for one and one for all**. Will DeMaurice Smith hold to the words that he said to Herb Adderley, with his arm around his shoulder, that the word retired would no longer be required—that from now on, union members are just union members?[15] Will he do more than appoint a former player/NFLPA member to sit at the negotiating table during the upcoming labor talks with the owners? Will Mr. Smith attempt to divert attention from the contemptible actions of the union leadership by seeking contributions*

15   Smith, "NFLPA Formally Announces Settlement in Herb Adderley Lawsuit."

*from the NFL to superficially satisfy his constituents' needs? Will he put forth a **legitimate** effort for all those concerned and clean up the way the union is operated and structured? Or will the union face a self-inflicted, self-destructive demise created by greed, egotism, and selfishness, which in turn breed unaccountability and disloyalty? In other words, will it seek and require in its new leadership the selfless sense of devotion, absent of greed, with a new, genuine, deep respect for all members, past and present? All members should join together equal in standing, equal in vision, with one purpose and one voice to achieve one goal. They must be an unbroken line.*

APPENDIX A

Research Provided by Barry Horn

Player Salaries and Compensation 2008

Players	Salaries
Quarterbacks	
Tony Romo	$4,574,099.00
James Brad Johnson	1,838,013.00
Brooks Bollinger	609,411.76
Isaiah Stanback	497,345.00
Defensive Line	
Greg Ellis	$3,606,239.65
Chris Canty	2,022,520.00
Jay Ratliff	1,817,162.00
Marcus Spears	1,528,020.00
Anthony Spencer	1,304,800.00
Terry "Tank" Johnson	825,000.00
L. P. Ladouceur	686,720.00
Stephen Bowen	450,520.00

Players	Salaries
Jason Hatcher	428,125.00
Marcus Dixon	88,400.00

Offensive Line

Leonard Davis	$5,171,706.00
Andre Gurode	3,673,386.00
Flozell Adams	3,103,703.00
Kyle Kosier	3,076,240.00
Marc Columbo	3,006,240.00
Montrae Holland	1,400,000.00
Joe Berger	933,249.00
Cory Procter	526,240.00
Doug Free	482,490.00
Pat McQuistan	465,990.00
Ryan Gibbons	83,200.00

Running Backs

Marion Barber	$2,522,400.00
Felix Jones	1,299,500.00
Tashard Choice	404,750.00
Deon Anderson	399,662.00
Alonzo Coleman	88,400.00
Julius Crosslin	88,400.00

Receivers

Terrell Owens	$5,723,228.00
Jason Witten	4,110,760.00
Patrick Crayton	2,206,120.00
Martellus Bennett	500,000.00
Austin Miles	456,228.00
Sam Hurd	454,094.00
Tony Curtis	450,760.00
Danny Amendola	88,400.00
Rodney Hamrick	88,400.00
Mike Jefferson	83,200.00

Players	Salaries

Linebackers

Players	Salaries
Bradie James	$3,356,120.00
DeMarcus Ware	2,163,240.00
Bobby Carpenter	1,760,760.00
Zack Thomas	1,255,760.00
Kevin Burnett	897,345.00
Justin Rogers	376,240.00
Tearrius George	88,400.00

Defensive Backs

Players	Salaries
Anthony Henry	$5,605,760.00
Roy L. Williams	4,627,302.00
Terrance Newman	3,617,263.00
Ken Hamlin	2,105,000.00
Mike Jenkins	1,146,000.00
Adam Jones	700,000.00
Keith Davis	645,000.00
Courtney Brown	392,125.00
Alan Ball	381,828.00
Orlando Scandrick	341,250.00
Pat Watkins	321,250.00

Kickers

Players	Salaries
Mat McBriar	$1,392,343.00
Nick Folk	403,720.00

The Cowboys vs. the NFL

(The first player listed under the league average is the highest paid at his position.)

Quarterbacks

League Average	$160,037
Archie Manning (Saints)	$600,000
Danny White	$235,000
Glenn Carano	$120,000
Gary Hogeboom	$45,000

Defensive Line

League Average	$92,596
Randy White (Cowboys)	$375,000
Ed Jones	$175,000
Harvey Martin	$165,000
John Dutton	$125,000
Larry Bethea	$70,000
Ron Spears	$60,000
Bruce Thornton	$45,000
Don Smerek	$35,000

Offensive Line

League Average	$65,543
Claude Minor (Broncos)	$226,250
Pat Donovan	$185,000
Howard Richards	$165,000
John Fitzgerald	$115,000
Herb Scott	$115,000
Tom Rafferty	$85,000
Glen Titensor	$75,000
Jim Cooper	$75,000
Andy Frederick	$75,000
Robert Shaw	$65,000
Kurt Petersen	$45,000
Norm Wells	$35,000
Steve Wright	$35,000

Running Backs

League Average	$94,948
Walter Payton (Bears)	$600,000
Tony Dorsett	$325,000
Robert Newhouse	$145,000
Ron Springs	$85,000
James Jones	$55,000
Timmy Newsome	$45,000

Receivers

League Average	$85,873
Lynn Swann (Steelers)	$340,000
Tony Hill	$135,000
Butch Johnson	$135,000
Drew Pearson	$125,000
Billy Joe DuPree	$115,000
Doug Donley	$100,000
Jay Saldi	$85,000
Doug Cosbie	$50,000

Linebackers

League Average	$85,205
Jack Ham (Steelers)	$299,667
Bob Breunig	$195,000
D.D. Lewis	$125,000
Guy Brown	$85,000
Mike Hegman	$75,000
Bill Roe	$45,000
Danny Spradlin	$45,000
Angelo King	$35,000
Anthony Dickerson	$35,000

Defensive Backs

League Average	$76,581
Mike Haynes (Patriots)	$241,666
Charlie Waters	$165,000
Randy Hughes	$135,000
Benny Barnes	$95,000
Dennis Thurman	$65,000
Steve Wilson	$65,000
Michael Downs	$39,000
Everson Walls	$37,000
Ron Fellows	$35,000
Dexter Clinkscale	$30,000

Kickers

League Average	$65,779
Mark Moseley (Redskins)	$143,000
Rafael Septien	$85,000

(These figures include base salary for 1981, deferred payments and any signing bonus owed the player for 1981. For example, Howard Richards, the Cowboys No. 1 draft pick last year, made $165,000 in his rookie year, with $105,000 as a bonus and $60,000 in salary. Randy White signed a new contract last year with a $200,000 base and a $75,000 signing bonus. Not included in the figures are performance bonuses and playoff money.)

— Gary Myers

Player Salaries and Compensation 1981
(*Dallas Morning News*, February 23, 1982)

APPENDIX B

An Explanation and Analysis of NFL
Disability Adjudication

"Anything that can go wrong will go wrong."
—Murphy's Law

"The NFL Disability Plan has been called the 'most generous and flexible' in all of professional sports by the *NFLPA White Paper (2007)* … [but] that is equivalent to saying that 'the slots at the South Point Casino are the most generous in Las Vegas.'"
—John Hogan, "NFL Disability: Illegal Procedure Revisited"

He didn't think it could happen to him—not to him. Brian DeMarco was a second-round draft star for the Jacksonville Jaguars in 1995; in 1999 the Cincinnati Bengals signed him to a $3.1 million contract; in 2007, at the age of 35, his spine was racked with disease and fitted with a titanium rod. He cannot work—let alone tackle for a professional football team. He cannot afford insurance. His medical expenses have rendered the star broke and his family homeless several times. The NFLPA, having assisted meagerly for a while, has deafened its ears to his pleas for help. No one is listening. He didn't think it could happen, but it can happen to anyone. It's happening all the time....

Attorney John Hogan, a prominent disability lawyer headquartered in Georgia, has handled a plethora of cases similar to DeMarco's. In his report on NFL Disability at the Las Vegas Independent Retired Players' Summit in 2009, Mr. Hogan reveals why disability benefits are so hard to obtain, and how the "Plan" not only violates a fiduciary duty to retired players, but violates the "spirit and intent" of ERISA Regulations. This book has revealed that players started with no benefits of any kind: no insurance, no retirement plan. To have gotten anything was a seemingly insurmountable task. But now, the little bit that has been won over the years has proven not to be even close to enough; the current "Plan" is a disgrace by modern standards.

It's one thing to point out that something violates all notions of fair treatment and decency; it's another to offer a solution. John Hogan has done just that. His 2009 report is reprinted here with his permission.

NFL DISABILITY:
Illegal Procedure Revisited
Independent Retired Players' Summit
Las Vegas 2009
by John Hogan, Attorney at Law

I.   Introduction.

Football is a game. Disability isn't. However, both need to follow explicit rules, or chaos ensues. NFL disability is in chaos.

The NFL Disability Plan has been called the "most generous and flexible" in all of professional sports by the *NFLPA White Paper (2007)*. However, that is equivalent to saying that "the slots at the South Point Casino are the most generous in all of Las Vegas." True, but both are equally difficult to win. In writing the *White Paper* for the NFLPA, Doug Ell of the Groom Law Group indicated that an employee of IBM or General Motors could not expect to obtain disability benefits decades after their employment ended. Again, quite true—but not many of their employees get tackled, sacked, clotheslined, or blindsided on a daily basis!

The scope of this presentation will be to explain the disability benefits offered under the Bert Bell/Pete Rozelle NFL Retirement Plan ("the Plan"); why they are so difficult to obtain; how they violate the spirit and intent of ERISA Regulations; where they violate the fiduciary duty owed to retired players; and some suggestions for meaningful changes and improvements.

II. Disclaimer.

As an attorney, I am obligated to set forth the following regarding this presentation:

1. I do not have all of the answers to problems with the Plan, as I do not have all of the information necessary to fully address those problems. Only a full and fair audit of the Plan by the Department of Labor or the GAO will disclose all of the information we seek about the operation of the Plan.

2. I am not an actuary. I do not know what my proposed changes would cost. However, the NFL and its member clubs are not GM, Chrysler, or a failing bank. Despite serious problems with the national economy, the value of each NFL team may be over One Billion Dollars, and there is no indication that player salaries, including untested rookies, are on the decline.

The cost of needed improvements to the Plan should surely be secondary to properly providing for the players who make the NFL clubs so profitable.

3. This presentation is only about the disability aspects of the Plan and does not discuss Pension or other important areas which also need significant improvement.

4. I do not wish the NFL to turn into the NFFL (National Flag Football League). Neither do I suggest that players should be expected to be paid for bloody noses, sprained ankles, personal faults and failures, nor the normal aches and pains that come with age.

III. Plan Basics.

The Bell/Rozelle NFL Retirement Plan is a joint venture between the NFL and the NFLPA. Plan Director, Sarah Gaunt, recently explained that the Plan is "neutral" between the League and the Union. The benefits office is located in Baltimore. The Retirement Board, which has the final say in disability determinations, is chaired by the NFL Commissioner, or his delegate—currently NFL VP Harold Henderson. It is comprised of six members: three appointed by the NFL Management Council and three by the NFLPA. Currently, those NFL members are: Dick Cass, President of the Baltimore Ravens; Clark Hunt, Owner of the Kansas City Chiefs; and William Bidwell, Owner of the Arizona Cardinals. The three NFLPA appointees are former players Tom Condon, Jeff Van Note, and Dave Duerson.

Initial Applications are determined by a two member Disability Initial Claims Committee ("DICC") comprised of Mary-ann Fleming, representing the NFL, and Chris Smith, representing the Union.

The Plan provides for two types of disability benefits: Line of Duty ("LOD") and Total and Permanent Disability ("T&P").

IV. Line of Duty Benefits.

A. Current criteria:

Paid to any player who incurs a "substantial disablement" arising out of League football activities. This is a strictly medical determination, using the American Medical Association *Guides to the Evaluation of Permanent Impairment*. For orthopedic impairments, the classifications are:

(a) a 38% or greater loss of use of the entire lower extremity;

(b) a 23% or greater loss of use of the entire upper extremity;

(c) an impairment to the cervical or thoracic spine that results in a 25% or greater whole body impairment;

(d) an impairment to the lumbar spine that results in a 20% or greater whole body impairment; or

(e) (any combination of the above) that results in a 25% or greater whole body impairment.

The monthly benefit amount payable for LOD is equal to the sum of the player's benefit credits or $1,500, whichever is greater.

Benefits are paid as long as the disablement lasts, but not longer than 7 ½ years.

Players do not need to be vested.

Player has to file application for LOD within 48 months of ceasing to be an active player; or, if longer, the number of credited seasons he played.

Benefit payable despite player's ability to work.

Will be offset by a higher paying T&P benefit.

B. Suggestions for Improvement:

1) Eliminate the 7 ½ year expiration. Pay benefit as long as impairment continues to exist.

2) Pay multiple benefit amounts for multiple impairments using the Veterans' Administration Service-Connected Disability Benefits model/ system.

* 10% disability might receive $1,000 per month.

* different body impairments can be rated separately—e.g., Ankle, knee, hip, spine, etc.

* 10% for ankle *plus* 20% for each knee *equals* 40 to 50% rating, which would pay $4,000 to $5,000 per month. (*Note: Under the VA system, percentages do not necessarily add up properly.*)

* Players who have a 60% to 70% combined disability rating, and who are not working, may apply for *unemployable status,* which if granted would give them 100% rating, which would be equal to full amount of T&P football degenerative benefit.

V. Total and Permanent Disability Benefits.

Must be an active or vested retired player. Defined as ***total disability to the extent that he is substantially prevented from or substantially unable to engage in any occupation or employment for remuneration or profit, but expressly excluding any disability suffered while in the military service of any country.***

Employment by the League; benevolent employment; and managing personal or family investments will not disqualify a player from T&P.

Categories and amount of benefits:

1) Active Football: Football related; within six months; Vesting not required; $224,000 per year

2) Active Non-Football: Not football related within six months; Vesting not required;

$134,000 per year or higher based upon benefit credits

3) Football Degenerative: Football related, within 15 years;

Must be vested;

$110,000 per year

4) Inactive: Not football related, no time limit;

Must be vested;

Not receiving NFL Plan retirement benefits.

VI. Focus on Football Degenerative Benefits.

A. Recent changes and "improvements":

(1) Deadline for proving disability changed from the later of 12 years after last credited season or age 45, to within 15 years of last credited season.

Congressional Research Service Report ("CRS") pointed out the fact that this can result in a significant age discrepancy for retirees at the 15 year deadline. Some vested players could be as young as 38 at the 15 year deadline; others as old as 65. In addition to the normal degenerative process increasing with age, this can be a determinative factor in Social Security disability claims. (CRS-81)

(2) Elimination of retroactive T&P benefits. Prior to a 2007 agreement signed by NFL VP Harold Henderson, and Gene Upshaw on behalf of the NFLPA, a disabled retired player might be eligible for up to 42 months of benefits.. Result could be as much as $375,000 less.

(3) Acceptance of favorable Social Security disability determination. Is now accepted as evidence that the retired player is totally and permanently disabled. NFLPA *White Paper* stated that in such cases, no examination by a Plan physician would be required, but my own experience indicates otherwise. (WP 6)

Current Case: Tight end Jimmie Giles played in the NFL for 13 seasons, making it to the pro bowl four times. He first applied for T&P in '96. The disability Plan's Medical Advisor Physician, whose opinion is binding, says that due to football injuries he is limited to sedentary work; therefore, under Plan rules, he is deemed "employable" and not disabled.

Jimmie subsequently took his early retirement from the Plan; but re-applies for disability under the Alliance "window" in 2008. He also applies for SSDI and is granted with an onset within 15 years of leaving the League. SSA determines that he cannot perform his past relevant work and has no transferable skills, and is limited to sedentary work. As he is over 50 at time of disability, he is disabled under SSA rules.

*Plan accordingly grants **inactive** T&P but wants to send to a neutral physician examination re: football degenerative. (Problems: It is now 4 years after the date of disability—current exam irrelevant; NFLPA White Paper— written by Plan attorneys— said that if SSA granted disability, Players would not* *have to be examined by a Plan physician.) Relying on the Union's position paper, Jimmie declined to undergo a purportedly unnecessary exam, and his claim for football degenerative benefits is denied. It is currently on further appeal.*

(4) Plan Medical Director.

May be an orthopedic whiz, but doesn't know disability law. (He cited medical evidence from 4 years after 15 year deadline to say Giles' total disability was not entirely football related—but due in part to obesity. Jimmie was medically obese when he played football–but obviously it did not stop him from a long and successful career. This determination is quite disingenuous, as when he underwent two examinations by the Plan's physicians in his 1996 application they never even recorded his weight!)

(5) Five year time frame until review—unless the Retirement Board thinks it should be sooner. (Suggested improvement: SSA's improvement standard.)

B. Other considerations:

(1) The CRS noted that the 15 year deadline appeared to be somewhat arbitrary. (Dave Pear, unsuccessful in his 1995 claim for T&P from the Plan, continued to work for several more years—taking outside sales jobs where he could vary his hours and lay down in his car before and after appointments. He could not hold out

any longer—17 years after his last season. Dave, the Tampa Bay Buccaneers' first all-pro, played in Super Bowl XV for the Oakland Raiders with a "broken neck." To date, he has had eight spinal surgeries and a hip replacement. He has surgery for the other hip scheduled in 2010, as well as an additional cervical fusion. Dave claims that he has paid more than $500,000.00 out of pocket for his football-related impairments.

There is absolutely no question that his total disability is football related.

It should also be noted that when Dave's 1995 application was denied, his Union offered no assistance or encouragement, instead telling him that the Plan would only grant his case if he were paralyzed and in a wheelchair!

(2) "Any occupation"—poorly defined. Literally? (Sell pencils on street?)

(3) What does totally disabled mean? Invalid? Full-time? Part-time? Seasonal? In a wheelchair?

(4) "Permanently" disabled can be ambiguous and confusing. (Ell's testimony to Congress mentions 12 month duration—but that's not in the Plan.)

(5) NEW—can be sent for a functional capacity evaluation at one of three facilities in U.S. NYC—Rusk Rehabilitation Institute. (If you are breathing, you have rehab potential?)

(6) The $110,000 benefit is, in fact, "generous." There is no offset for other disability benefits (SSDI), as is common for LTD cases.

VII. Comparison of T&P to other disability programs.

A) Social Security.

(1) Difference between SSDI and SSI. Disability Insurance v. Federal Welfare.

(a) SSDI—*Disability Insurance*

Same "pocket" as retirement benefits. For wage earners who become disabled prior to retirement age.

Deadline to become disabled up to five years after stopping work.

Monthly benefit for minor children 50% of PIA.

Medicare for wage earner after 24 months of entitlement.

Retroactive benefits for up to 12 months from application. (But prior application can be re-opened for up to four years for good cause such as new and material evidence.)

No limit on resources. (Thomas "Hollywood" Henderson, of Cowboys fame, was on disability from the Plan, but taken off after he won the Texas lottery. However, it appears that the cessation was not due to this extra income, but due to the fact that he was working as a motivational speaker, and making quite a lot of money from that.)

Nine month trial work period—unlimited earnings.

Can work if less than "substantial gainful activity" ($980 mo. Gross).

Can apply for disability even though receiving early RSI.

Can be offset by Workers' Compensation (80% pre-disability limit).

(b) SSI—*Supplemental Security Income*

"Federal Welfare" for disabled. Very strict income and resource limits.

No benefits for family.

No retro. (Two years to R&R)

Medicaid.

(c) *Definition of Disability:*

The inability to engage in any substantial gainful activity by reason of any medically determinable physical or mental impairment which has lasted or can be expected to last for a continuous period of 12 months or result in death.

The impairment(s) needs to be so severe as to preclude past relevant work, and any other work which exists in significant numbers in the national economy considering age, education, and work experience.

If SGA, medicals not even considered.

If not SGA, SSA has medical conditions which are considered disabling without consideration of whether the claimant could be expected to perform past work or other work. *(Suggestion: If player has two separate impairments which would qualify separately for a grant of LOD—grant T&P. For example—when Dave Pear's T&P was denied, the Plan doctor said that he had an 80% or greater impairment to his spine. That is 3–4 times the rating which is required for LOD—SHOULDN'T HE BE ENTITLED TO SOMETHING WITH THAT SEVERE A SPINE??*

Focus is on inability to perform full-time work. (Social Security Ruling 96-9P)

If over 50, and unable to perform past work, and no transferable skills, is considered disabled at the sedentary level. (55—light) (Problem for the Plan? Used to saying that someone limited to sedentary is employable and not disabled!?)

If under 50—ANY full-time job.

"Hiring practices" not considered. (Rate of pay; job openings)

Drug or alcohol abuse may preclude payment.

Opinion of treating physician(s) may be controlling. Consulting exams may be undertaken if enough info not available from treating sources, or there is a conflict. (Under the Plan, treating physician reports are ignored, and the reports of the Plan's doctors are controlling.)

B) **Long Term Disability (Group Insurance under ERISA).**

Generally need to file claim while employed (although may be on sick leave).

General definition: *(for the first 24 months) Inability to engage in all the material duties of your own occupation by reason of illness or injury. After 24 months, disabled to the point of being able to perform any occupation you are reasonably suited for based upon training, education and experience.*

Generally pays 60 to 70% of base monthly salary/earnings for the 12 months prior to commencement of disability. (OT, bonuses excluded)

24–48 month limit on payment for "mental and nervous" or "self-reported illnesses" (fibromyalgia).

Reduced by other disability income. (WC, SSDI)

May work at reduced role/part-time to test ability to work; and/or some offset, but not cessation of benefit.

"Any occupation" generally at the same salary as LTD benefit and jobs need to actually be available.

As burden to prove disability is upon claimant, emphasis is on treating medical sources. May send for an Independent Medical Exam if more info is needed or to resolve conflict.

VIII. Disability Process under the NFL Plan.

A) **Application**

A retired player must file a written application

with the NFL Player Benefits office to begin the disability claim process. The application seeks basic information such as what injuries are claimed and whether they are football related. The player is also asked about employment information. While the answers to the questions may seem routine and straight-forward, to someone suffering from severe chronic pain, or the common symptoms of mild traumatic brain injury, the task may be all too daunting. (I still don't understand why the NFLPA, their union, does not assist players in some way with the application process.)

B) Player sent for *neutral physician examination*. Has become mandatory, although Plan document indicates it is discretionary. (Sec. 5.2) May be sent for several.

Neutral asked whether medical conditions are football related;

Whether player is "totally and permanently disabled" and if not,

What kind of work they can perform.

C) Disability Initial Claims Committee ("DICC") evaluation.

DICC comprised of two voting members, one from the NFL Management Council (Mary-ann Fleming) and one from the NFLPA (Chris Smith) (or their designees).

Teleconference meetings with guests and advisors.

May table for additional neutral examinations.

Case is granted if both DICCs vote in favor; Denied if both vote against.

Case is deemed denied if there is a split vote.

Player is sent written notification of denial; has 180 days to appeal to the full Retirement Board.

IX. Violations of ERISA and Fiduciary duty.

(1) Neutral physicians.

Are they truly neutral? How selected? How trained? When dismissed? (*Two clients saw same doc in Texas who said they were totally disabled—he was soon off the panel. WHY??*)

All other disability plans use treating sources as the main source of information to evaluate a disability case.

The Plan paid the Groom Law Group over $147,000 to write two similar briefs to the U.S. Supreme Court to argue against the mandatory adoption of Social Security's *treating physician rule* in ERISA cases. Although the Dept. of Labor did not find any legal fault with this, I find it highly offensive to retired players that the Plan would take a stand against adopting a law that might have made it somewhat easier for some retired players to qualify for disability.

SSA's treating physician rule provides that *If we find that a treating source's opinion on the issue(s) of the nature and severity of your impairment(s) is well-supported by medically acceptable clinical and laboratory diagnostic techniques and is not inconsistent with the other substantial evidence in your case record, we will give it controlling weight.*

It does not mean that your disability needs to be granted just because one of your doctors says so. If the treating doctor's opinion is well supported by objective evidence and there is no substantial, credible evidence to the contrary, *why wouldn't the Plan want to grant his disability?*

(2) Insufficient and ambiguous information from the neutral physicians.

How many minutes/hours can a player walk/sit/ stand at one time, and in total during an eight-hour day?

Do they need to have the freedom to alternate sitting and standing at their discretion? Do they need to have the ability to lie down at unscheduled times?

Do they take medications that might interfere with their ability to pay attention, concentrate, and respond to changes in the work setting?

How much can they lift and carry? Can they squat, crouch, kneel, and bend without limits?

Are there any limitations on using their hands and fingers to reach, feel, grasp, and perform fine manipulation?

A medical doctor is not trained to give an expert opinion on what occupations, if any, a person might perform.

(3) **Failure to consider vocational factors.**

Just because a player might be capable of sedentary work does not mean that they are employable—as the Plan commonly finds. There is no consideration of age, education, experience, etc., which are real-world factors in whether a person is actually employable.

(4) **Violation of fiduciary Duty of Care.**

Section 8.8 of the Plan provides that: *"The Retirement Board and the DICC will discharge their duties with respect to the Plan and Trust solely and exclusively in the interest of the Players and their beneficiaries, and with the care, skill, prudence, and diligence under the circumstances then prevailing that a prudent man acting in a like capacity and familiar with such matters would use in the conduct of an enterprise of like character and with like aims."*

In other words, disability under the Plan should be undertaken in a similar manner to other disability programs where the definition of disability—i.e., the inability to work—is similar. *THEY'RE NOT DOING IT!*

(5) **Failure to follow ERISA time limits in adjudicating cases.**

When the U.S. Department of Labor published ERISA claim reforms in the *Federal Register* in 2000, they set strict guidelines for disability determinations at the initial claims decision stage and upon review. Over the objections of many groups and insurance companies who indicated that disability claims were complicated and might take a lot of time to resolve, the Dept. of Labor stated that: "speedy decision making is a crucial protection for claimants who need either medical care or the replacement income that disability benefits provide."

Section 11.6 of the Plan reflects the strict time limits required for a determination to be made as required by ERISA—but they ignore them when it suits their purposes.

(6) **Failure to follow the spirit and intent, if not the letter, of ERISA regulations in deciding a claim at the DICC level and in communicating the denial to the Player.**

Basic fiduciary law (and the Plan itself) provides that the DICC members owe a duty of care and loyalty to the players and their beneficiaries; and that they not act in an arbitrary or capricious manner. However, we are all aware of numerous stories of the NFL Management Council members voting to deny a claim or ordering further neutral examinations in spite of fully favorable medical opinions from their own carefully chosen neutral physicians. Certainly they are empowered, and even required, to do so if the opinion is unsupported or unreasonable. However, they routinely do so just because they can. Or, if they have a legitimate reason, it is never explained.

The loyalty is not to the NFL or Union—it is to the player and the trust fund. If votes to grant, deny, or delay are routinely made along party lines—one side or the other—fiduciary duties are being violated.

Similarly, the denial decisions issued by the DICC generally ignore the ERISA requirements to give specific reasons for the adverse determination; and make a mockery of the requirement to inform the player of the additional information or material necessary for him to perfect the claim and an explanation of why such material or information is necessary.

Federal Courts have held that disability claims are not meant to be endurance contests.

A proper denial decision should briefly recite all of the medical evidence and other material considered in making the decision; discuss how each was evaluated and where the claim fell short. I am not sure that each of the DICC members has seen all of the evidence submitted on a claim, let alone know how it was evaluated.

It appears that the reason for this is that regardless of what the player submitted in support of his claim, it generally rises or falls solely upon one or more opinions of the neutral physician. Similarly, they do not feel the need to tell the player what additional information might be necessary to perfect (i.e., win) his claim, because that does not matter, as on appeal he will be sent for one or more additional examinations.

In the NFLPA's *White Paper*, the Groom Law Group wrote "*On appeal, the player is sent, as required by federal law, to one or more new neutral physicians for additional medical examinations.*"

Doug Ell has repeated this assertion in testimony before Congress.

FEDERAL LAW (ERISA) DOES NOT REQUIRE ANY NEUTRAL PHYSICIAN EXAMINATIONS!!!! This interpretation is a bastardization of ERISA regulations that require that on appeal, any medical professional consulted shall not be the subordinate of any such medical professional who was consulted at the initial claim level. It does not require an examination. It also presupposes that the opinion was unfavorable—and thus the claim was denied. However, the Plan often denies claims in spite of favorable opinions.

The Plan should explain what the player would need to provide to perfect his case. Does he need an updated MRI? A range of motion examination? And it should certainly spell out, in detail, why they have rejected the opinion(s) of any treating or neutral physicians. *Not an unsubstantiated assertion that there is a conflict.*

(7) Do the members of the DICC and Retirement Board have the skill they are required to possess to adjudicate disability claims?
I'm not sure they know the difference between an asshole and an elbow!

When I pressed them for an explanation of why they disregarded the report of a Board Certified Neuropsychologist—regarding the cognitive limitations of a player who had numerous concussions—they wrote that it was because he was not an M.D.

In Dave's case, when they saw that he had an 80% or greater impairment to his spine, they should have known enough to disregard the opinion that he could work; or seek further information or clarification or another opinion.

Anyone can vote "yes" or "no" when they do not have to provide an evaluation and analysis of the evidence in a disability claim—particularly where they can do so without any justification whatsoever.

Disability is not a game. It is not supposed to be a roll of the dice, nor is it a gauntlet to be run.

D) Appeal to the full Retirement Board.

(1) Deadline is 180 days from DICC denial notice.
(2) Player sent for additional neutral exam(s).
(3) Upon deadlocked vote of Board, claim is sent for a binding examination by a Medical Advisory Physician. **("MAP")**

As name indicates, is supposed **to advise, not examine.**

Under Sec. 11.4 (b) MAP should decide if additional tests or exams are required—not the Board.

Violation of ERISA duty of care on the part of the Board members to defer a binding opinion to the MAP.

Violation of ERISA Regulations in that Board must give a full and fair review to all evidence, arguments, materials submitted on appeal: negated by one binding exam.

Also routinely violate ERISA requirements for timely decisions.

E) **Appeal beyond the Retirement Board.**

Final administrative determination of the Plan.
Appeal to the U.S. District Courts—42 month limit.

F) **Why Are Most Plan Decisions Upheld in Federal Courts?**

(1) ERISA law prevails.
(2) No jury.
(3) Record is closed at time Board issues decision.
(4) Reservation of Discretion by Plan causes courts to review for abuse of discretion—do not retry case; will not overturn Board decision even if the preponderance of the evidence mitigates against it.
(5) Federal courts hate to be bothered by individual disability cases.

X. NEEDED IMPROVEMENTS TO THE SUBSTANCE AND PROCESS OF THE NFL DISABILITY PLAN.

(1) Eliminate the Reservation of Discretion clause so that U.S. D.C. can review final decisions under the normal burden of proof—preponderance of the evidence.
(2) Adopt Social Security's treating physician rule.

(3) Hire adjudicators who have the knowledge and experience to evaluate disability claims themselves.

(4) Seek much more detailed information from treating and examining physicians on the limits a player has as the result of his impairments.

(5) Consider the vocational factors needed to properly assess employability.

(6) Adopt an improvement standard for cessation of disability.

(7) Adopt some specific guidelines for part-time or occasional work or trial work attempts.

(8) Allow players who have taken retirement to subsequently apply for disability.

(9) In a tip of the hat to Brent Boyd—fire the Groom Law Group.

(10) Continue to press Congress for a full and fair audit of the Plan.

Bibliography

Berry, Robert C., William B. Gould, and Paul D. Staudohar. *Labor Relations in Professional Sports*. Dover, MA: Auburn House Publishing Co., 1986. 126–141. Print.

Blaudschun, Mark, and Gary Myers. "Team Doctors Are Caught Between Their Employers and the Athletes They Treat." *Dallas Morning News* 11 July 1982: B. Print.

Elias, Paul. "Jury Orders NFL Union to Pay $28.1M to Retirees." *Associated Press* 10 Nov. 2008, Print.

Hogan, John. "NFL Disability: Illegal Procedure Revisited." Las Vegas Independent Retired Players Summit, 2009: Print.

Horwitch, Lauren. "Company Set Up by SAG's Allen Under Fire." *Backstage.com* 1 Aug. 2007: Web. 21 Aug. 2008. 8/21/08 accessed at http://www.backstage.com/bso/esearch/article_display.jsp?vnu_content_id=1003619163

"Jeff Nixon Sports Report: Tony Davis and the Retired Player Advocates." Voice America Sports. Web. 23 Mar. 2009. http://www.modavox.com/voiceamerica/vepisode.aspx?aid=37216

Kopf, Spencer W. "Garvey Garbling Player Issues." *Dallas Morning News* 11 July 1982: 4B. Print.

Masteralexis, Lisa P., Carol A. Barr, and Mary A. Hums. *Principles and Practice of Sport Management.* 3rd ed. Sudbury, MA: Jones and Bartlett, 2009. 417. Print.

Myers, Gary. "Dutton's Disgusted." *Dallas Morning News* 30 Jul. 1982: B. Print.

Myers, Gary. "The Cowboys vs. the NFL." *Dallas Morning News* 23 Feb. 1982: B. Print

Smith, Heath. "NFLPA Formally Announces Settlement in Herb Adderley Lawsuit." *NFLPLAYERS.COM* 5 Jun. 2009: Web. 6 Nov 2009. http://www.nflplayers.com/user/content.aspx?fmi d=178&lmid=443&pid=3540&type=n&weigh=443,0,3540,n

Wilner, Barry. "New NFLPA Exec Working Without Contract." *ABCNews.go.com* 22 Apr. 2009: Web. 6 Nov 2009. http:// abcnews.go.com/Sports/wireStory?id=7405279

Winner, Christopher P. "Fairfax Clears 2 Redskins In Rape Probe." *Washington Star* 24 Oct, 1980, Print.